CW00323805

Portugal

Portugal

Text by Neil Schlecht
Revised by George McDonald
Photography: Chris Coe
Cover photograph by Chris Coe
Layout: Media Content Marketing, Inc.
Cartography by Raffaele De Gennaro
Managing Editor: Tony Halliday

Eleventh Edition 2002

NO part of this book may be reproduced, stored in a retrieval system or transmitted in any form or means electronic, mechanical, photocopying, recording or otherwise, without prior written permission from Apa Publications. Brief text quotations with use of photographs are exempted for book review purposes only.

CONTACTING THE EDITORS

Every effort has been made to provide accurate information in this publication, but changes are inevitable. The publisher cannot be responsible for any resulting loss, inconvenience or injury. We would appreciate it if readers would call our attention to any errors or outdated information by contacting Berlitz Publishing, PO Box 7910, London SE1 1WE, England. Fax: (44) 20 7403 0290;
e-mail: berlitz@apaguide.demon.co.uk

All Rights Reserved

© 2002 Apa Publications GmbH & Co. Verlag KG, Singapore Branch, Singapore

Printed in Singapore by Insight Print Services (Pte) Ltd, 38 Joo Koon Road, Singapore 628990. Tel: (65) 6865-1600. Fax: (65) 6861-6438

Berlitz Trademark Reg. U.S. Patent Office and other countries. Marca Registrada. Used under licence from the Berlitz Investment Corporation

050/211 REV

CONTENTS

Portugal

PORTUGAL AND THE PORTUGUESE

F ew countries have risen as triumphantly or fallen as far
as Portugal. From preeminent global superpower in the
16th century, with far-flung colonies and abundant riches, to
forgotten backwater of Continental Europe, Portugal is again
a country and society in transition.

As part of the newly integrated Europe, Portugal has raced
to catch up to its neighbors. Parts of the country are suddenly modern and cosmopolitan, while just as much remains
stubbornly traditional. Visitors will find stunning modern
architecture and fashions in Lisbon and Porto alongside
women decked out head-to-toe in traditional black mourning
dress. On rural roads just outside the capital and across the
country, families still trudge along behind wooden oxcarts.
Not since the rubble was cleared from the Great Earthquake
of 1755 has the contrast between old and new been greater.

Following the Reconquest of Iberia by Christians, daring
Portuguese explorers set out in caravels from the Algarve.
Rounding Africa's Cape of Good Hope and eventually
reaching India and the Pacific, as well as the Americas and
Brazil, they ushered in a dramatic Age of Discovery.
Opening world trade routes across the globe, explorers
established Portugal as a maritime superpower; spices, gold,
and diamonds flowed across the seas to Lisbon.

Portugal soon lapsed into decline, tattered by wars and
constitutional crises, and for two centuries or more the country remained isolated from the rest of Europe.

Portugal's storied history has left an inescapable imprint
on both the land and people. The Phoenicians came to trade,
the Romans established roads and cities, the Jews built syn-

agogues, and the Moors left great citadels, almond orchards, and whitewashed villages of labyrinthine alleyways. The inhabitants of the northern regions reveal Germanic and Celtic origins in their blue eyes and fair skin, while the dark eyes and olive complexions of the Moors and their plaintive style of singing can still be seen and heard in the south.

Like Ireland and Spain, Portugal has long waved goodbye to emigrants who've set off for Germany, France, and the US in search of economic opportunity. As the Portuguese economy has improved, though, many have returned. Evidence of wealth earned abroad is visible in new home construction in many small towns throughout Portugal, but predominantly in the north. Since relinquishing control over its former

The capital city of Lisbon, as viewed from the Moors' old castle, Castelo de São Jorge.

colonies in Africa and Latin America, a democratic and stable Portugal has also received waves of immigrants. These new arrivals add a vital element of cultural diversity on the streets of Lisbon and other cities.

Today travelers are discovering more of the varied treasures of Portugal, even though most still stick to the sunny beaches of the Algarve or the sophisticated city life of the capital, Lisbon. Though Portugal's most celebrated destinations are among the highlights of Europe, those willing to venture beyond the most familiar haunts will be richly rewarded. Portugal—less than half the area of Britain, roughly the same size as Indiana, and home to just 10 million people—has hundreds of unique attractions, is surprisingly easy to explore, and offers an astounding variety of landscapes within relative proximity. Even a short trip allows one to see a great deal.

Rebuilt after the devastating earthquake of 1755, Lisbon has charming neighborhoods that reflect the city's Moorish roots and spectacular vistas. The city straddles innumerable hills and the Tagus, the mighty river that flows from Spain across central Portugal. Though Lisbon has long been considered a laid-back provincial city, it is now a thriving European capital.

With about 160 km (100 miles) of coastline, the Algarve is one of Europe's premier beach destinations. Its abundant sports, beaches, hospitable weather, and easily organized package vacations attract as many visitors as the rest of Portugal combined. The blocks of tourist apartments and hotels and meticulously manicured golf courses are atypical for the country, but the coast remains true to its hype. International and Portuguese sun-seekers venture south for long, glorious stretches of golden sands, secluded coves framed by odd ochre-colored rock formations, and deep green waters.

North of the Algarve lie the flat agricultural plains of the sun-scorched Alentejo, home to Évora, a stunning small city founded by the Romans. Stretching to the Spanish border are historic castles perched on clifftops, vast estates, small whitewashed villages, and fields of wheat, olives, and cork oaks. The unhurried pace is a welcome contrast to the tourist-mad enclaves farther south.

The regions Estremadura and Ribatejo extend north of Lisbon along the Atlantic and into the central plains. It is a land of coastal fishing villages, beaches, agricultural towns hugging the Tagus river, and grand religious monuments, such as the abbeys of Alcobaça and Batalha, the famed shrine at Fátima, and the Convento de Cristo in Tomar. It is also the site of impressive castle-topped towns, like picture-perfect Óbidos.

Farther north is the varied landscape of the Beiras, a land of forests, the Serra da Estrela mountain range (the country's highest and home to the famous serra cheese) and more picturesque, fortified towns. The region is home to seaweed collectors of the coastal lagoons, mountain shepherds, and the students at the university in Coimbra, Portugal's great intellectual center.

The far north looks and feels very different from southern and central Portugal. It is lush, green, and starkly traditional. Rather than olives, cork, oranges, and almonds—the main crops cultivated in the south—the Douro Valley is dotted with magnificent terraced vineyards that produce the grapes for the country's centuries-old port wine. The wine is shipped from river-hugging *quintas* (estates) to cellars in Vila Nova de Gaia, across the river from Porto, Portugal's second largest city. Porto was once mainly an industrial, workmanlike city, but it now claims a revitalized cultural scene and is fascinating in its own right.

The Minho, north of Porto, includes the ancient state of Portucale, which later lent its name to the country as a whole. The region, perhaps Portugal's most beautiful, contains the lush Peneda-Gerês National Park and several historic gems, including the towns Braga, Guimarães (Portugal's first capital), and Viana do Castelo, which doubles as a popular coastal resort.

Tucked away in the northeastern corner is Portugal's most remote and perhaps most unusual region: Trás-os-Montes (literally "beyond the mountains"). In this land long reputed to be the haunt of witches and wolves, traditional mores continue much as they have for centuries. The sparsely populated region especially appeals to hikers, who come to explore the many beautiful parks, wild moorlands, isolated villages, and dramatic citadels in historic towns such as Bragança and Chaves.

Magnificent year-round weather has transformed parts of Portugal, particularly the Algarve, into a huge destination for sporting vacations. Superb golf facilities abound—several with tees dramatically clinging to cliffs and just skirting the edge of the ocean—and horseback riding, tennis, big-game fishing, sailing, and windsurf-

Fresh produce abounds in agriculture-rich Barcelos.

ing are immensely popular. Stunning beaches can be found all along the coast, not just in the Algarve—though the waters can be downright chilly up north. Along the west coast are a number of spots offering fine sport fishing and world-class surfing.

Portugal is rarely lacking for exuberant local festivals and street markets. Whole villages come to life, with everyone taking part, from the youngest children to venerable grandmothers dressed in traditional black. More sophisticated affairs—trendy

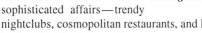

Fishing boats in Tavira bring in the staples of Portuguese cuisine.

nightclubs, cosmopolitan restaurants, and lively bars—can be found in the larger cities.

But this part of the world, at the western edge of Europe, is best discovered at an unhurried pace. One of the great joys is enjoying Portuguese cuisine and wine, whether at a simple country inn or a chic new spot in Lisbon or Porto. Predictably, local cooking owes much to the country's close ties to the sea: fresh fish, seafood, and soups hearty enough for a tired sailor's homecoming. Many people are familiar with Portugal's famed port wines, which come from the north, but one of the country's great secrets are the table wines produced in the Alentejo, Dão, and Douro regions. They're affordable, unpretentious, and memorable —which, come to think of it, is not a bad description of Portugal itself.

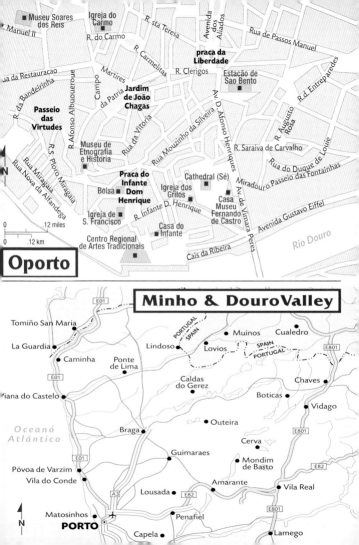

Oporto

- Museu Soares dos Reis
- Igreja do Carmo
- R. do Carmo
- Manuel II
- R. sta Teresa
- Avenida dos Aliados
- Rua de Passos Manuel
- R. Carmelitas
- praca da Liberdade
- Martires
- R. Clerigos
- Estação de Sao Bento
- Rua da Restauracao
- R. da Bandeirinha
- Campo da Patria
- Jardim de João Chagas
- Rua Afonso Albuquerque
- R.d. Entreparedes
- Av. D. Afonso Henriques
- R. Augusto Rosa
- R. Saraiva de Carvalho
- Rua da Vitoria
- Rua Mouzinho da Silveira
- Museu de Etnografia e Historia
- R.S. Pioro Miragaia
- Rua Miragaia
- Rua Nova da Alfandega
- Praca do Infante Dom Henrique
- Rua do Duque de Louie
- Miradouro Passeio das Fontainhas
- Cathedral (Sé)
- Bolsa
- Igreja dos Grilos
- Casa Museu Fernando de Castro
- Igreja de S. Francisco
- R. Infante D. Henrique
- Av. de Vimara Peres
- Avenida Gustavo Eiffel
- Casa do Infante
- Passeio das Virtudes
- Centro Regional de Artes Tradicionais
- Caís da Ribeira
- Rio Douro

0 — .12 miles
0 — .12 km
N

Minho & Douro Valley

- E01
- Tomiño San Maria
- PORTUGAL SPAIN
- Muinos
- Cualedro
- La Guardia
- Lindoso
- Lovios
- SPAIN PORTUGAL
- E801
- Caminha
- Ponte de Lima
- Caldas do Gerez
- Chaves
- Viana do Castelo
- Boticas
- Vidago
- Oceaño Atlántico
- Braga
- Outeira
- Cerva
- E801
- Guimaraes
- Mondim de Basto
- Póvoa de Varzim
- Vila do Conde
- A3
- Lousada
- E82
- Amarante
- Vila Real
- E801
- Matosinhos
- PORTO
- Penafiel
- Capela
- Lamego
- E82
- N

A BRIEF HISTORY

The early history of Portugal is closely related to that of the entire Iberian peninsula. Prehistoric cultures flourished first in the north and in today's Alentejo region of south-central Portugal. The south was visited by a number of peoples who came primarily to trade, including the Phoenicians, the Mycenaean Greeks, and the Carthaginians. The Phoenicians established a trading post at Lisbon around 1200 B.C, calling it either Alis Ubbo or Olissipo. When Celtic peoples crossed the Pyrenees in the first millennium B.C., they intermarried with the existing Iberian population and built a series of hilltop fort communities or *citânias*, the finest example of which is at Briteiros (see page 73).

The remains of a Roman temple in Évora are testament to the city's early occupants.

The Carthaginians, under Hannibal, recruited locals to fight as mercenaries against Rome. The Romans eventually defeated the Carthaginians and invaded the Iberian peninsula. Their occupation was fiercely opposed by a confederation of Celts, known as the Lusitani, living in central Portugal. The Lusitanian leader, Viriathus, kept the Roman forces at bay until he was assassinated in 139 B.C.

The Romans cultivated grapes, wheat, and olives; built roads; and bequeathed the Latin foundations of the Portuguese language and a strong base of Christian belief. Julius Caesar founded many cities, including Ebora (Évora), where the remains of a Roman temple survive (see page 90), and Pax Julia (Beja).

The Moors and the Reconquest

In A.D. 711 a great Muslim invasion fleet from North Africa crossed the Strait of Gibraltar. In a matter of only a few years, the Moors had conquered almost all of Iberia, except for the small Christian kingdom of Asturias in northern Spain. Lisbon became a thriving outpost under Muslim occupation.

The Moors failed to penetrate much further north than Aveiro about halfway up the Atlantic Coast. They settled in the Alentejo, along the Tagus river, and in the Algarve (which they named al-Gharb, or "Western Land"). By the mid-ninth century, al-Gharb had become a Moorish kingdom, with a capital at Chelb, or Silves, (see page 107).

The Moors introduced new crops, including oranges and rice, to the region. Their highly distinctive whitewashed houses and filigree chimneys are features of Portugal to this day, as are azulejos (handpainted, glazed ceramic tiles). Many Moorish place names also survive, including that of Fátima, the pre-eminent Catholic site in Portugal. Unlike their successors, the Moors were tolerant of the many different peoples who lived together in Portugal, including Berbers, Arabs, Christians, and Jews.

Even so, the Moors were regarded as an occupying power by the local Christian population. The Christian Reconquest, which sought to drive the Muslims out, was under way in the north by the ninth century.

It was not until 1128, when Dom Afonso Henríques became the Count of Portucale, that the struggle to regain power met with any real success. Henríques consolidated his position by defeating the Moors at the Battle of Ourique in 1139, and celebrated by naming himself the first king of Portugal.

By 1185 the frontier between Christianity and Islam had been drawn at the Tagus. Not until 1249 did King Afonso III (1248–1279) complete the Reconquest and secure borders

The Moors left a number of their imposing castles scattered across the country, including this one in Silves.

for Portugal — 250 years before the Spanish could do the same.

Consolidation and Golden Age

Afonso III moved his capital from Coimbra to Lisbon in 1260, six years after he had called the first *Cortes* (parliament) in Leiria. His successor, Dom Dinis (1279–1325), consolidated Portugal's borders by constructing castles along the frontier with Castile.

The last of the Afonsin dynasty, King Fernando I (1367–1383), formed an alliance with the English and appealed for support in his disputes with Spain. When Fernando died without an heir, the Spanish

Henry the Navigator, through his far-flung expeditions, altered the very way that Europeans viewed the world.

claimed the throne through a web of intermarriages between the two royal houses. Spain was backed by Portuguese aristocrats, eager to avoid war.

The army of Juan I of Castile invaded Portugal in 1383, but João of Avis, recently proclaimed King João I of Portugal, defeated the Spaniards in a decisive battle which was fought in 1385 at Aljubarrota, about 100km (62 miles) north of Lisbon. Batalha Abbey (see page 45) was built in gratitude. The victory secured independence from Spain. A new alliance with England was sealed in the 1386 Treaty of Windsor; a year later João of Avis married Philippa of Lancaster, the daughter of John of Gaunt. Their third surviving son, the Duke of Viseu, Master of the Order of Christ, would change the map of the world. Ultimately he become known as Henry the Navigator.

Building an Empire

With Portugal facing the Atlantic Ocean , rather than the Mediterranean Sea, it remained cut off from most trade routes. However, as the Ottoman Turks in the 15th century dominated the Mediterranean and shipbuilding technology improved, longer Atlantic journeys became a serious prospect. Peace with Spain in 1411 prompted Portugal

The historic Mosteiro dos Jerónimos holds the remains of Vasco da Gama.

to seek overseas conquests.

Prince Henry retired to what was known as the "end-of-the-world," the Sagres peninsula in the Algarve (see page 101). There he established a school of navigation that attracted astronomers, cartographers, and other leading scientists of the day. Henry established expeditions that ultimately succeeded in redefining Europeans' very understanding of the world. During Henry's lifetime, Portuguese caravels sailed far beyond the westernmost point of Africa. With the colonization of Madeira and the Azores, the foundations were laid for the future Portuguese empire. The Portuguese also sailed down the west coast of Africa, even going beyond Cape Bojador in 1434, a feat theretofore considered to be impossible.

Henry died in 1460, but Portugal's discovery voyages continued. The king who ruled over the golden age of exploration — and exploitation — was Manuel I "The Fortunate," who reigned from 1495–1521. The many important discoveries that were made during his reign would assure his position as Europe's richest ruler: He could well afford to erect monuments as elegant as the Tower of Belém and as impressive as the Jerónimos Monastery in Lisbon.

King João I ordered the construction of the massive Battle Monastery in 1385.

The architecture that eased Portugal from the Gothic into the Renaissance still bears his name: the Manueline style is whimsically flamboyant and decorative, and rife with references to the sea.

The most significant expedition under Manuel's flag was Vasco da Gama's legendary sea voyage from Lisbon in the summer of 1497—immortalized in *The Lusiads* (1572), the epic poem by Portugal's national poet, Luís de Camões (1524–1580). Rounding what is now known as the Cape of Good Hope, da Gama found what Columbus had been searching for in 1492 (although in the wrong direction): the sea-route to the lucrative spices of the East. The Portuguese thus ended the Venetian monopoly on Eastern trade and began attracting merchants from all over Europe to Lisbon.

Portugal and Spain, the planet's foremost maritime powers, agreed to divide the world between them by means of the 1494 Treaty of Tordesillas. This accorded everything lying more than 370 leagues west of the Cape Verde Islands to Spain, while everything lying to the east went to Portugal, thus giving Portugal a free hand in exploiting the Orient. In 1500, Portuguese explorer Pedro Álvares Cabral accidentally reached Brazil.

Trading posts were set up all along the west and east coasts of Africa, in the Middle East (Hormuz),

The Torre de Belém was erected in 1515 to defend the entry to Lisbon.

southern India (Goa), Malaysia (Malacca), and even in China (Macau). Profits came primarily from trading in eastern spices, silk and porcelain, African gold, and slaves, as well as through importing copious sugar from Brazil and São Tomé.

Wealth helped disguise inherent weaknesses in the Portuguese state. It was not long before other nations, such as the English and the Dutch, began challenging the Portuguese monopoly on the spice trade.

No entrepreneurial class developed, as it did in Holland and England. The only real entrepreneurs were the Jews, who were forced either to embrace Christianity or face expulsion. The Inquisition took root in the 1530s, and the

The Monument to the Discoveries depicts Henry the Navigator leading a procession of noted explorers, astronomers, and map-makers who supported his mission.

Counter-Reformationary Jesuit order gained control of education in Portugal during the 1560s.

The general population was sorely depleted, many having left for the new colonies. When the king (and cardinal) Dom Henrique died leaving no heir in 1580, King Philip II of Spain marched in and, backed by wealthy Portuguese, forced the union of the two crowns.

Spanish Rule and Restoration

Philip II of Spain became Filipe I of Portugal in 1581. Philip upheld Portuguese autonomy, making no attempt to unite his two kingdoms. It took 60 years for the Portuguese to organize a successful uprising against the occupation. On 1 December 1640—a date still celebrated as Portugal's Restoration Day—Spanish rule was finally completely overthrown. The Duke of Bragança was crowned King João IV in a festive ceremony that took place on Lisbon's beautiful riverfront square, the Terreiro do Paço (today the Praça do Comércio).

His grandson, João V, enjoyed a long and glittering reign (1706–1750). As money poured in from gold discoveries in Brazil, the king spent it on lavish monuments and buildings (including the spectacular aqueduct that still brings fresh water into the center of Lisbon). Portugal's citizens, overburdened with taxes, bore the brunt of the king's extravagances.

Destruction, Rebuilding, and the Peninsular War

The middle of the 18th century marks a great divide between early history and modern times in Portugal. On All Saints' Day, 1 November 1755, as crowds packed the churches to honor the dead, Lisbon and parts of Portugal all the way to the Algarve were devastated by one of the worst earthquakes ever recorded. Churches crumbled, the waters of the Tagus heaved into a tidal wave, and fires spread throughout the city. The three-dimensional disaster is estimated to have killed between 15,000 and 60,000 people—a trajedy of immense proportions.

The task of rebuilding fell to the power behind the throne, an ambitious and tyrannical minister known as Sebastião José de Carvalho e Melo, best remembered as the Marquês de Pombal. Pombal dominated Portugal as an enlightened despot, banishing the Jesuits and executing certain members of the nobility who may have been involved in an assassination attempt on the king. He abolished slavery, reformed

Pilgrimage site in Fátima, where the Virgin Mary was spotted in 1917.

education, and diversified Portuguese trade. Although he lost his hold on power shortly after José's death in 1777, many of his reforms survived, laying the foundation for the modern Portuguese state.

At the beginning of the 19th century, Napoleon managed to drag Portugal into the heat of Europe's conflicts. France invaded in 1807 when Portugal refused to close its ports to British shipping. The royal family fled to Brazil aboard a British ship and the British general, Arthur Wellesley (later the Duke of Wellington), countered the invasions. The final battle came in 1810–1811, when the French, unable to pass the huge fortifications at Torres Vedras, retreated back to Spain.

The Fall of the Monarchy

In 1814 Portugal made peace with France, and Brazil was raised to the status of a full kingdom the following year. Portugal itself was ruled as a virtual British protectorate. A military coup in 1820 finally persuaded João VI to return to Portugal in 1821 and agree to a new constitution.

Peace proved elusive, though, and the country was again torn by war—this time pitting brother against brother. Pedro IV, previously emperor of Brazil (which had asserted its independence from Portugal), fought to wrest the crown from Miguel I, his absolutist brother. Pedro won, though he died of consumption only months later at the age of 36. His adolescent daughter, Maria da Glória, assumed the throne.

Widespread discontent arose from continued government instability, futile attempts to modernize the economy, and coffers depleted from the cost of maintaining overseas colonies. Republican idealists led a failed coup in 1891. The government declared itself bankrupt in 1892, and emigration reached unprecedented levels. Finally, in 1908, King Carlos and his eldest son, Luís Filipe, were assassinated as they rode in an open carriage through the Praça do Comércio (see page 31) in Lisbon. The younger son survived to become King Manuel II, but he was deposed merely two years later and forced to flee to Britain, thus ending over 750 years of monarchy.

The Republic and the New State

The new republic was unable to provide the stability Portugal needed. Governments changed no less than 45 times between 1910 and 1926, and the country's disastrous involvement in the First World War led to economic chaos. After a revolution in 1926, General António Óscar Carmona assumed control, two years later entrusting the economy to

---

Manueline Architecture

The Portuguese may be principally known for azulejo designs and port wine, but equally important is the ornate style of architecture and stone carving that suddenly appeared in Portugal in the late 15th century. It flourished for only a few decades, for the most part coinciding with the reign of Manuel I (1495–1521), for which it was christened "Manueline."

Probably triggered by the great ocean voyages of discovery, it took late Gothic as a base and added fanciful decoration, dramatic touches that were frequent references to the sea. Stone was carved like knotted rope and sculpted into imitation coral, seahorses, nets, and waves as well as non-nautical designs. The style first appeared in the small Igreja de Jesus in Setúbal (see page 41) and Lisbon's Torre de Belém (see page 35) and Mosteiro dos Jerónimos (see page 36). The style reached a peak of complexity in the unfinished chapels of the monastery at Batalha (see page 45). You can also see exuberant Manueline stonework all over the Algarve; look for the church portals and windows at Silves (the Igreja da Misericórdia), Alvor, and particularly at Monchique. In the 16th century, the style fell out of favor and by 1540 Portugal had joined with the rest of Europe in building in the more sober Renaissance style.

António de Oliveira Salazar, an economics professor at Coimbra University. The exhausted Portuguese finances immediately perked up.

In 1932 Salazar was named Prime Minister. His austere authoritarian regime—the *Estado Novo* (New State)—favored economic progress and nationalism. He kept Portugal neutral in World War II, but permitted the Allies to use the Azores as a base.

Toward the Present

Salazar's New State began to unravel when Portugal's former colonies demanded independence. In 1974, soldiers carrying red carnations in their rifle barrels successfully deposed the government in a peaceful coup that came to be known as the "Carnation Revolution." Portugal then disengaged itself from Mozambique and Angola, its seething colonial possessions in Africa, and the country absorbed the million or so refugees who fled to a motherland most had never seen.

Portugal suffered several years of political confusion, but stable democracy finally took hold. With its entry into the European Union (formerly the European Economic Community) in 1986, the pace of development suddenly quickened. With aid from the EU, Portugal became one of the fastest-growing countries in Europe. In 1998, Portugal hosted the World Expo in Lisbon. Pope John Paul II paid his third visit to the shrine of Fátima in 2000 and beatified (the final step before sainthood) the shepherd boy and girl who claimed to be visited by the Virgin Mary over a period of six months in 1913.

In 2002, Portugal abandoned the escudo and joined most other members of the European Union in adopting the euro as its everyday currency.

WHERE TO GO

A lthough a small country, Portugal is blessed with incredible geographical diversity. Carved out of the western sixth of the Iberian peninsula, the country is quite easy to get around. Even a relatively short amount of time and distance covered allows visitors to sample varied regions and attractions, including famed beaches, rugged mountains, splendid castles, traditional rural villages, and gorgeous medieval cities. Most visitors still focus on the charming capital, Lisbon, and the alluring sunny beaches of the Algarve, but there's much more to Portugal.

 ## LISBON

For years Lisbon has enjoyed a reputation as a relatively quiet town, without the hustle, bustle, and general hassle of other major European cities. While there are still ample remnants of that easy-going charm, the gap is quickly closing; the city now hardly lacks for traffic and noise.

Portugal's capital city is the country's largest, with a population of more than 2 million. Due to a massive earthquake that obliterated much of the ancient city, most of the architecture that remains is from the 18th century. However, old sections of the town survive in the winding alleys of the medieval and Moorish district, known as the Alfama. (The city is covered in greater detail in the Berlitz POCKET GUIDE TO LISBON).

The center of Lisbon is small, compact, and easy to get around in just a few days. The city is built on hills—by legend seven, but in fact many more—providing several splendid vantage points. Perhaps the best place to start your tour of Lisbon is from the Moors' old castle, the **Castelo de São Jorge**. The fall of the castle to crusaders in 1147 proved cru-

cial in the Reconquest of Portugal from the Moors. From its ramparts you can take in the whole of the city and the broad Rio Tejo (River Tagus), spanned by the longest suspension bridge in Europe.

Alfama & Baixa districts

Nearby, the atmospheric medieval **Alfama** district is Lisbon's most picturesque and fascinating area. It spills down the side of a hill between the Castelo de São Jorge and the Tagus with all the color and bustle of an Arab bazaar. The *bairro* (district), in fact a legacy of the Moors, is a charming labyrinth of crooked streets, cobbled alleyways, decaying old houses and palaces, fish stalls, and *fado* music clubs. The Alfama was one of the few areas to survive the earthquake.

Another majestic view of the city is from a charming park, **Miradouro de Santa Luzia,** just down the hill from the castle. Lisbon's **Sé Patriarcal** (cathedral) appears out of nowhere at a bend in the road (most easily reached from the center by continuing east on the extension of Rua da Conceição). Begun as a fortress-church in the 12th century, its towers and walls suggest a beleaguered citadel. Adjacent to the cathedral is the

The Pantheon dominates the skyline of the medieval district of Alfama.

lovely **Igreja de Santo António da Sé**, named for Lisbon's patron saint, St. Anthony of Padua.

Just beyond the dense quarters of the Alfama is **São Vicente de Fora** (St. Vincent Beyond the Walls), an Italianate church and monastic cloister. The latter is the true highlight: Its courtyards are lined with blue-and-white azulejos and the views from the roof are among the best in the city.

Down toward the river is the **Museu Nacional do Azulejo** (National Azulejo Museum), devoted entirely to the art of painted and glazed ceramic tiles, a national art form. About 12,000 are on display here, from 15th-century polychrome designs to 20th-century art deco styles. A prized possession is the *Lisbon Panorama*, a 36 m- (118 ft-) long tile composition of Lisbon's riverside as it looked before the 1755 earthquake. Part of the museum, which occupies a former convent, is the fabulous interior of the small church of **Igreja da Madre de Deus,** a heady mix of gilt Rococo and gorgeous azulejos.

> *Azulejos* are the hand-painted, glazed ceramic tiles that are omnipresent in Lisbon.

A district known as the **Baixa** (Lower City)—the low-lying area between hills on either side—was devastated by the great earthquake of 1755. The Marquês de Pombal supervised the city's reconstruction, redesigning it according to a geometric grid of broad avenues.

The Baixa is Lisbon's principal business district. **Praça do Comércio**, a grand square with a vast triumphal arch, is lined on three sides by gracious arcaded buildings. The square (also called by its former name Terreiro do Paço), wholly wiped out by the great earthquake of 1755, has seen its share of watershed political events: King Carlos and his son were felled by an assassin's bullets there in 1908, and it was the site of one of the first uprisings of the Carnation Revolution of 1974.

Ferries ply across the Tagus from a point near the square, and from another to the west near the **Cais do Sodré** railway station, where trains depart for Estoril and Cascais.

A wide pedestrian shopping street, **Rua Augusta**, leads from the Praça do Comércio through a stately arch to the central square of Lisbon, Praça Dom Pedro IV, better known as the **Rossio** (the Common). Once the scene of bullfights, it now hosts a funfair and is a popular meeting point, ringed by cafés. The National Theater is located here, and across the road is the **Estação do Rossio** (with trains to Sintra and other places)**,** which looks something like a Moorish palace with horseshoe arches, just west of the square. Two blocks north is another lively square, **Praça dos Restauradores**, with its historic obelisk commemorating the overthrow of Spanish Hapsburg rule in 1640. The main tourist office is located here at Palácio Foz, on the west side of the square.

The broad and leafy Avenida da Liberdade runs for 1 km (0.6 mile) north, flanked by gardens, ponds, and fountains, as far as the circular Praça Marquês de Pombal (also known as the

The sidewalk cafés on Rua Augusta offer a place to rest without missing the action.

Rotunda), where a statue of the dictator Pombal gazes over the city.

North of Parque Eduardo VII, off Avenida António Augusto Auiar, is Lisbon's most remarkable museum, **the Museu Gulbenkian.** One of the finest private collections in Europe (since bequeathed to Portugal), it was created as an exhibiton space for the thousands of works of art acquired by the renowned Armenian billionaire Calouste Gulbenkian. A little further north you'll find the impressive 18th-century **Aguas Livres Aqueduct**, which still carries water along its 18-km (11-mile) length to a point near the modern Amoreiras Shopping Center.

Praça dos Restauradores is marked by this distinctive commemorative obelisk.

Bairro Alto & Belém

Back toward the river, and just west of the Praça do Comércio is **Lapa**, an elegant residential neighborhood. Its standout attraction is the **Museu Nacional de Arte Antiga** (National Museum of Ancient Art), Portugal's largest museum. Among its masterpieces of international renown are *The Adoration of St. Vincent,* a multi-panel work attributed to the 15th-century Portuguese master, Nuno Gonçalves, and *The*

Temptation of St. Anthony, a fantastic hallucination by Hieronymus Bosch, tempered with humor and executed with mad genius.

The **Bairro Alto** (Upper City) is a hilly area full of evocative houses decorated with wrought-iron balconies usually occupied by birdcages and flowerpots. At night the district is loaded with atmosphere: patrons tumble from restaurants, theaters, bars, and *fado* clubs. It's a relatively harmless place by day, but you should exercise some care after dark.

Perched on the edge of the Bairro Alto is one of Lisbon's most evocative sights, the shell of the 14th-century **Igreja do Carmo**, which was packed with worshippers on All Saints' Day, 1755, when the terrible earthquake brought the roof down. The church remains deliberately preserved as an atmospheric ruin. Nearby, the sumptuous 16th-century **Igreja de São Roque** features a lavish baroque chapel of São João Baptista (St. John the Baptist) and a small museum of sacred art.

You can easily walk to the Bairro Alto from the central squares in the Baixa, but it's also fun to go by tram or board the landmark 30-m (98-ft) **Elevador de Santa Justa**,

The Elevador de Santa Justa remains a well-used landmark in the Bairro Alto.

which you'll find just off Rossio square. The stately elevator, a 1902 Victorian marvel of iron and glass, was built by Raul Mesnier (not Gustave Eiffel, as many continue to believe). The longer, slower route back downhill meanders through the elegant shopping area of **Chiado**, now totally rebuilt after a drastic 1988 fire that swept through the district.

Some 6 km (4 miles) west of Praça do Comércio along the river lies the riverside district of **Belém**. Many of the great voyages of discovery set out from here in the 15th and 16th centuries. The new sea routes produced a golden age of commerce, and

Manueline architecture is glorified in the Mosteiro dos Jerónimos in Belém.

King Manuel built two magnificent monuments to commemorate the country's achievements.

Tram 15 makes the waterfront trip to Belém from Praça do Comércio, as do buses no. 29 and no. 43.

One is the small but exquisite **Torre de Belém,** a romantic medieval fortress (particularly when floodlit by night) erected in 1515 to defend the entry to Lisbon and one of the finest examples of Manueline architecture (see page 25).

The majestic Palácio Nacional de Sintra contains many of the oldest and most valuable azulejos in Portugal.

By contrast, the majestic **Mosteiro dos Jerónimos** is Lisbon's largest religious monument and a truly formidable example of Manueline architecture. The imposing church and its double-decker cloister miraculously survived the 1755 earthquake. In addition to royal tombs, the monastery holds the relics of national heroes Vasco da Gama and the poet Luis de Camões. It also houses an archaeology museum, and next door is the **Museu da Marinha** (Naval Museum).

Back down the street toward Lisbon is the highly popular **Museu Nacional dos Coches** (National Coach Museum), located in the former riding school of the Belém Royal Palace.

One of Belém's best-known symbols is the modern **Padrão dos Descobrimentos** (Monument to the Discoveries). The huge waterfront sculpture depicts Prince Henry the Navigator at the prow of a stylized caravel jutting into the Tagus River. The figures just behind Prince Henry represent noted explorers, map-makers, and astronomers whom he mobilized in order to launch Portuguese ships into the history books.

Other attractions in Belém include the Gulbenkian Institute's **Planetarium** and the huge **Centro Cultural de Belém,** home to concerts and art exhibits.

Eastern Lisbon

At the extreme opposite of the city, Lisbon's newest attraction is the park designed for the World Expo '98, which did much to reinvigorate the faltering industrial section in the eastern part of the city. Continuing to draw visitors to the riverfront **Parque das Nações** (Nations Park) is its world-class aquarium, the **Oceanário de Lisboa,** perhaps the world's top aquarium. The park is a little out of the way, but easily accessible by Metro (subway).

The Palace Gardens at Palacio Nacional de Queluz are the pride of the region.

LISBON ENVIRONS

Queluz

Just 14 km (8 miles) west of Lisbon is the **Palacio Nacional de Queluz,** home to the pretty pink palace commissioned by Pedro III. The sumptuous summer palace was built in the second half of the 18th century as an official working residence for the royal family. The Palace Gardens are the pride of Queluz, with clipped hedges in perfect geometric array, imaginative fountains, and armies of statues.

☞ Sintra

Though Sintra, 30 km (18 miles) to the northwest of Lisbon, suffers the effects of its enduring popularity, it is one of the finest towns in Portugal to visit. Nestled into the Serra de Sintra, 25 km (16 miles) northwest of Lisbon, it

was once a coveted summer retreat for royals and today is a romantic getaway for people from all over the world. Clustered throughout the forested hillsides are old palaces and estates with spectacular vistas.

Located right in the center of town is the spectacular **Palácio Nacional de Sintra** (also called the Paço

The Palácio de Pena is a crazy hodgepodge of architectural styles and details.

Real, or Royal Palace), easily recognized by its two huge, white conical chimneys. Used since the early 14th century as a stately summer home for Portuguese kings, its interiors and furnishings are remarkable, including one of the oldest and most valuable collections of azulejos to be found in all of Portugal.

> **Most museums in Portugal are closed on Monday, but Queluz takes Tuesday off— and any other day when visiting heads of state are in residence.**

A steep road of hairpin turns leads up into the serra from Sintra to the town's most spectacular monuments. The oldest is the **Castelo dos Mouros** (Moors' Castle), erected during the 8th century soon after the Moors occupied Portugal. The dauntless Afonso Henriques conquered it for the Christians in 1147, a major victory in the reconquest of Portugal. Those with the energy to do so should climb the ramparts to the top for incredible views of the entire forested area.

On the hilltop further up the same winding road, over 450 m (1,500 ft) above sea level, is the **Palácio da Pena**, an outrageous Victorian folly built in 1840. The palace is a bizarre and extravagant cocktail of Gothic, Renaissance, Manueline, and Moorish architecture fashioned as a love nest for Queen Maria II (1834–1853) and her smitten husband, Ferdinand of Saxe-Coburg-Gotha. Inside, rooms are a riot of imaginative, ornate, and in some cases suffocatingly sumptuous, details.

A short hop from Sintra are the attractive village of **Colares**, the beach at **Praia das Maçãs,** and the rugged coastline at **Cabo da Roca**, the westernmost point of the European mainland. Sintra's helpful tourist information office, on Praça da República in the old quarter, can direct you to any of these.

Estoril Coast

The Costa do Estoril (formerly called the Costa do Sol) begins just west of Lisbon and goes all the way around the tip of the peninsula to Guincho on the open Atlantic. Those seeking pollution-free swimming (see page 132) usually head for **Guincho**, but the famous old resort of Estoril itself, some 24 km (15 miles) from Lisbon, is still worth a visit. The beaches and resorts west of Lisbon are all accessible by train from the capital's Cais do Sodré station.

While Estoril is a full-scale resort—cosmopolitan and sybaritic—**Cascais**, which sits on a pretty curved bay, leads a double life, as a town of fishermen and kings, where the humble and the retiring rich coexist with camera-toting tourists.

The Ponte 25 de Abril, over the River Tagus, will put you on the path to many popular destinations south of Lisbon.

The main square is a charmer. The **Paços do Concelho** (Town Hall) has stately windows with iron railings, separated by panels of azulejos depicting saints. A forbidding 17th-century fort, known as the **Cidadela** (citadel), is one of the few buildings to have survived the earthquake and tidal wave of 1755. The municipal park down the road holds the **Museu dos Condes de Castro Guimarães**, a museum with archaeological remains, art works, old furniture, gold, and silver.

The road west (3 km/2 miles from Cascais) passes **Boca do Inferno** (Mouth of Hell), a geological curiosity where, in rough weather, the waves send up astonishingly high spouts of spray accompanied by ferocious sound effects.

At **Guincho**, you have the choice of either a sandy beach or the rocks to fish from, but be careful: They face the open sea and it's often rough.

South of the Tagus

The **Ponte 25 de Abril**, across the River Tagus, became the longest suspension bridge in Europe when it was opened to traffic in 1966. It leads to several destinations south of Lisbon popular with Portuguese and international visitors alike.

The topographical highlight of the Arrábida peninsula is undoubtedly the **Serra da Arrábida** (site of a nature reserve), a mountain chain around 35 km (22 miles) long which protects the coast from the strong north winds and accounts for the Mediterranean vegetation. The tiny little beach spot, **Portinho da Arrábida,** is popular with Portuguese weekenders.

Setúbal, the district capital, is just a 20-minute drive from Lisbon by motorway, longer if you take the picturesque route via Sesimbra and Arrábida. This is olive and citrus country, with cows grazing among the trees. Setúbal is a conglomeration of market town, industrial center, resort, and Portugal's third largest fishing port.

Setúbal's greatest historical and artistic treasure, the Gothic **Igreja de Jesus**, was built around 1490 by the great French architect Boytac, who later built Lisbon's glorious Jerónimos Monastery (see page 36). A dramatic main portal leads into the church, which boasts two inspired elements of decoration: 17th-century azulejos on the walls, and stone pillars like twisted strands of clay, fragile-looking in spite of their obviously solid dimensions.

North of Lisbon

In modest Portugal, the dimensions and extravagance of the convent and palace of **Mafra**, 40 km (25 miles) to the northwest of Lisbon, are quite staggering. The riches are attributable to King João V, who in 1711 conceived this project to celebrate the long-awaited birth of his first child, Princess D. Maria, after three years of marriage. The convent took 13 years to build and employed more than 50,000 people at one time. Its huge cost gave rise to a Portuguese saying that João transformed the diamonds of Brazil into the rocks of Mafra.

The convent library is the undisputed highlight; it has a vaulted ceiling, a precious wood floor, and tall shelves housing 30,000 books, making it the largest one-room library in Portugal. Visits to the Mafra Palace are by guided tour only (English-speaking at 11am and 2:30pm daily; closed Tuesday), and last about an hour.

Another 10 km (6 miles) to the coast is the fishing village and growing resort of **Ericeira,** a natural port. The old section is a winsome town of cobbled streets winding between white-washed cottages, everything clean, neat, and treasured by both inhabitants and visitors alike.

ESTREMADURA AND RIBATEJO

The historic regions north of Lisbon—Estremadura, between the Tagus river and the Atlantic coast, and Ribatejo, extending into the agricultural central plains—possess some of Portugal's most important monuments and most interesting and attractive towns.

Óbidos & the Coast

Almost too perfect to be true, the high medieval walls of **Óbidos** completely encircle a jewel of a town. Equally hard to believe, this inland town was once a port and *coastal* fortress until the sea inlet here silted up, leaving the quiet Óbidos lagoon cut off and the shoreline nearly 10 km (6 miles) away.

Traditionally the town was given as a wedding gift from the King of Portugal to his bride. An entrance at the north end is guarded by the 13th-century castle, which has been adapted as one of the more luxurious and perennially full *pousadas* (see page 174). The narrow streets inside the town's walls are enchanting, all lined with white-washed houses decorated with colorful flowers. It's a safe bet that Óbidos has never looked so neat and clean in all its history, so it's inevitably jammed with curious visitors at times.

At street level, Rua Direita, the main drag, runs from one gate to the other. Just down from the castle, the parish church, **Igreja de Santa Maria**, has handsome blue 18th-century azulejos, an odd blue-painted ceiling, and the gilded tomb in the north wall. Afonso V married his cousin Isabel in this small church in 1441, when they were mere children (he was 10, she all of eight).

Due west on the coast, the old port of **Peniche** was once an island. The port's imposing fortifications were built by

Intricate azulejos festoon the Mosteiro de Santa Maria de Alcobaça (above), built to celebrate an 1147 military victory over the Moors. Mosteiro da Batalha (right) also commemorates battle supremacy.

Spain during its period of rule in the 16th century. The fishing harbor is usually jammed with colorful, storm-battered craft and flanked by excellent informal fresh fish restaurants. The fort nearby held political prisoners during the Salazar régime; now it's a museum as well as a display area for local crafts and traditions. In fine weather you might wish to take a trip to the island of **Berlenga**, 12 km (7 miles) offshore. With monastery ruins and an impressive 17th-century fort that still stands, it's now a sanctuary for seabirds.

Alcobaça and Batalha Abbeys

Two admirable abbeys—and two of Portugal's most moving monuments—are found inland north of Óbidos. The first is the former Cistercian monastery **Mosteiro de Santa Maria de Alcobaça**. Built to celebrate a victory, the 1147 battle in which Dom Afonso Henriques took over the town of Santarém from the Moors, the church remains the largest in Portugal.

In the transept, about 30 m (100 ft) apart, are the tombs of Pedro I and Inês de Castro, their effigies facing each other and surrounded by attendant angels. Pedro and Inês lived a tragic love story that ended with her murder—ordered by Pedro's father, King Afonso IV. The lovers' tombs are decorated with Portugal's greatest medieval stonecarving. The monastery's so-called Cloister of Silence, ordered by King Dom Dinis in the early 14th century, is a model of harmony and simplicity.

Farther north (16 km/9 miles) is the even more impressive, many-turreted and buttressed **Mosteiro da Batalha** (Battle Monastery). King João I ordered the construction of this Gothic masterpiece in gratitude for the victory over Juan I of Castile at the Battle of Aljubarrota nearby in 1385 (see page 17).

In the center of the Capela do Fundador (Founder's

The Royal Cloisters are among many wonders to behold at Mosteiro da Batalha.

Chapel), a tomb contains the remains of João and his queen, Philippa of Lancaster; their effigies lie side by side, hand in hand. Family members are nearby—niches in the walls hold the tombs of their children, most notably that containing Prince Henry the Navigator.

Portugal's Unknown Soldiers are buried in the monastery's Chapterhouse. This vaulted chamber, 20 sq m (65 sq ft), was a great engineering wonder in its day (around 1400). Due to fears that the unsupported ceiling would collapse at any time, the architect is said to have employed only convicts under sentence of death to work on the project.

Be sure not to miss the unfinished chapels, open to the sky, at the east end of the church but visited from the outside.

The quintessential fishing village **Nazaré,** the Portuguese "Nazareth," is now a thriving commercial resort. However, some fishermen here continue to wear the colorful local dress, black stocking-caps and plaid trousers, and the women still appear in black shawls, bright aprons, and seven petticoats (one for each day of the week).

Sítio, the 90-m (300-ft) cliff at the north end of Nazaré, offers an excellent vantage point over the green hilly countryside, the tiled

The neo-Baroque basilica of Fátima is said to be twice as big as St. Peter's in Rome.

roofs of the neatly packed town, and mile after mile of beach open to the full force of the Atlantic Ocean.

Fátima

Set in bleak hill country about 135 km (84 miles) north of Lisbon, **Fátima**—once just a poor village—is one of the most important centers of pilgrimage in the Catholic world, along with Lourdes in France and Santiago de Compostela in Spain.

On 13 May 1917, three young shepherds claimed they saw a series of miraculous visions of the Virgin Mary—said to disclose three secrets, or prophecies, to the children—followed by a solar phenomenon witnessed by thousands in October of the same year. (Two of the children died of pneumonia soon after these inexplicable events; the third, Lucia, now in her 90s, has been a cloistered Carmelite nun in Coimbra since 1929 and makes very few public appearances.)

The 20th-century neo-Baroque basilica that draws so many of the faithful, said to be twice as big as St. Peter's in Rome, faces an immense but rather plain square. Pilgrimages are held on the 13th of every month, with the most important observances on that date in May and October. Yet even on an ordinary weekday, scattered believers, some kneeling in penitence, come to Fátima to pay homage to the Virgin Mary.

Tomar

Sitting astride the River Nabão, **Tomar** (34 km/21 miles east of Fátima) is one of Portugal's most fascinating towns.

Tomar's pleasant central square, **Praça da Republica**, is flanked by the elegant Manueline church of São João Baptista, with an unusual octagonal belfry and intricate portico, and the 17th-century town hall. The statue in the center of the plaza tells the real story of the town, though. Beneath a colony of ever-present pigeons, it depicts Gualdim Pais, Grand Master of the Portuguese branch of the crusading Order of the Knights Templar, to whom the town was granted in 1157.

Unusual for a town so dominated by Christian crusaders, a small 15th-century **sinagoga** (synagogue) survives on Rua Dr. Joaquim Jacinto, just off the main square. The room has a high vaulted ceiling, along with eight clay pots embedded in the walls to improve the acoustics (classical concerts are now occasionally held here). A museum displays old Jewish tombstones. In 1992, Yom Kippur was celebrated here for the first time in 500 years.

The standout sights, however, are up on the hill above town. The Templars' old stronghold, the UNESCO World Heritage sites **Castelo dos Templários** (Templars' Castle) and the accompanying **Convento do Cristo** (Convent of Christ), overlook Tomar from wooded heights. Behind crenellated walls, the outstanding 12th-century Convento do Cristo is one of the highlights of central Portugal.

At the heart of the complex is the original Templar church, the fascinating 12th-century Charola, a 16-sided structure based on the Church of the Holy Sepulchre (built over Christ's tomb) in Jerusalem. Knights once attended services here on horseback. In its interior is a gilded octagonal structure, which appears almost more pagan than Christian-looking. Recently completed restoration has revived the Charola's esoteric paintings. The two-storied nave, added by Manuel I, is divided into an upstairs choir and a chapterhouse underneath.

One of the finest Manueline windows in Portugal is carved in the western wall of the Chapterhouse, encrusted with profusely carved marine motifs. The grand Renaissance-style Claustro Principal (Great Cloister) was added in the 16th century.

Halfway up the wooded road to the Convento de Cristo is the 16th-century **Ermida da Nossa Senhora da Conceição**, a handsome little basilica in classic Italian Renaissance style.

From Tomar an enjoyable excursion is to the fairytale castle at **Almourol**, marooned on an island in the Tagus. Just upriver is **Abrantes,** with its own castle overlooking the town.

Santarém, 78 km (48 miles) northeast of Lisbon, is the ancient capital of the agricultural region of the Ribatejo, whose lifeblood is the mighty River Tagus.

Few of Santarém's monuments have survived, although the Jesuit seminary and church on the main square, the triangular Largo Sá da Bandeira, has an impressive 17th-century baroque façade. North of the city center is the 15th-century **Igreja de Graça,** with its magnificent Gothic rose window, amazingly carved from a single piece of stone. In the south of the city is the Marvila church, built in Manueline style, with fine 17th-century azulejos. Across the street is an interesting archaeological museum in a Romanesque church.

A fine panoramic view can be had from the **Portas do Sol** *miradouro* (belvedere), a garden surrounded by Moorish walls overlooking the River Tagus and the extensive plains of the Ribatejo. A Phoenician dye house was recently discovered on the grounds.

In this agricultural land, bulls and horses can be seen grazing all over the Ribatejo. **Vila Franca de Xira** (45 km/28 miles down the Tagus in the direction of Lisbon) is a modest town, but the center of Portuguese bullfighting. Every July and October, a festival with Pamplona-style bull-running through the streets (called a *largada*) accompanies the bullfights.

The tranquil town of **Golegã** explodes once a year, when the important Feira Nacional do Cavalo (National Horse Fair) is held in November. If you can't be here when all the horses and breeders are, at least have a look at the fine portal of the 16th-century Igreja Matriz and a couple of small art museums in town, one the remarkable Museu de Fotografia Carlos Relvas.

Numerous migratory birds can be seen in the **Tagus Estuary Natural Reserve,** an important wetlands whose headquarters are in **Alcochete**.

The Beiras

The three ancient provinces known as the Beiras together make up the broad swathe of land lying between the Tagus and Douro rivers. Beiras means "edge," revealing the boundary position these provinces have long occupied between northern and southern Portugal. Each of the three provinces retains its own distinctive character.

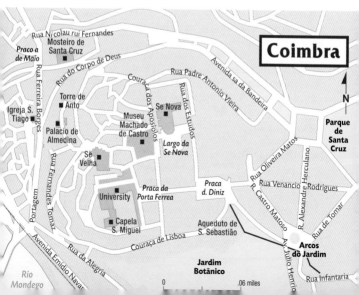

The lovely university city of Coimbra dominates the **Beira Litoral** (Coastal Beira). The neighboring coastline forms part of the Costa de Prata (Silver Coast) and has largely escaped development, though it does have resorts at Figueira da Foz and Aveiro.

Inland is the spectacular terrain of the **Beira Alta** (Upper Beira). Small granite hills begin to develop into great mountains dressed in pine trees. The population is small and the number of tourists few, despite the strange beauty of the landscape, with its giant boulders and flowery meadows. The **Serra da Estrêla** is the backbone of the area and offers a host of wonderful valleys and waterfalls for hikers, fortified by the area's fabulous cheese.

Further south, the mountains give way to the agricultural plains of the **Beira Baixa** (Lower Beira), which lacks the monuments and mountains of its neighbors, but still maintains an unspoiled way of life.

Coimbra and Around

The magnificent university city of **Coimbra,** the country's capital during the 12th and 13th centuries, has been the pillar of Portuguese intellectual life since 1290. Today it is a lively and prosperous city, swimming with students.

The famous **Universidade de Coimbra** is the country's oldest. The university sits on top of a hill in the old town, high above the River Mondego. Wending their way up to the University are several small streets that hide *repúblicas* (halls of residence similar to fraternities and sororities) and numerous small bars that reverberate to the strains of Coimbra's own distinctive version of *fado* (see page 128).

The principal courtyard of the University is marked by a belltower and surrounded by historic buildings on three sides. At one end is the spectacular baroque **Biblioteca Joanina** ☛

(library), constructed in 1720 with João V's Brazilian wealth (also instrumental in building the great library at Mafra; see page 42). Three exquisitely gilded and painted chambers house some 300,000 leather-bound texts in many languages. On the same side of the courtyard are the **Museu de Arte Sacra** (Museum of Sacred Art), recently closed for restoration, and **Capela de São Miguel** (St. Michael's Chapel), with fine azulejos and a massive baroque organ. Directly ahead is the highly ornate ceremonial hall, the **Sala dos Capelos**, the heart of university life (it's where degrees are given out).

The nearby **Museu Nacional de Machado de Castro**, housed in the former archbishop's palace, exhibits an excellent collection of medieval sculpture and religious paintings. Among the museum's complex of historic buildings are a Moorish tower and Roman crypt in a fascinating warren of underground passages.

On either side of the museum are Coimbra's two cathedrals, the classical-baroque **Sé Nova** (New Cathedral) and the vastly more interesting **Sé Velha** (Old Cathedral). The fine Romanesque bulk of the old cathedral is reminiscent of the early crusading cathedrals of Lisbon and Porto. Renaissance detail has been added around the portals, but the interior remains fairly stark. A chapel to the right contains a collection of impressive life-size stone carvings of Jesus, Mary, and the Twelve Disciples. Be sure not to miss the peaceful Romanesque cloister.

The single-nave **Igreja de Santa Cruz,** built in 1131, is renowned for its dazzling Manueline detail, including an elaborate portico and carved pulpit. The church holds the tombs of Portugal's first and second kings, Afonso Henriques and Sancho I, and the Claustro del Silencio (Cloister of Silence) is lined with pretty arches and colorful azulejos. Down towards the river, the **Jardim Botânico**, with plants collected from across Portugal's far-flung empire, is Portugal's largest.

Across the river are the **Convento de Santa Clara-a-Velha** (Old St. Claire Convent, long under extensive restoration aimed at rescuing it from the river), where the lifeless Inês de Castro was crowned (see page 45), and the newer, uphill **Convento de Santa Clara-a-Nova** (New Convent), where the silver tomb of Isabel, the sainted queen of Dom Dinis, is located. Nearby is the **Quinta das Lágrimas** estate, now an elegant hotel, where Inês was reputedly murdered. Legend holds that the garden's "pool of tears," immortalized in the epic poem by Luis de Camões, is stained deep red by the actual blood of the doomed 14th-century lover.

Also on the south side of the river is a good spot for families: **Portugal dos Pequinitos**, a children's theme park where many of the country's greatest and most typical buildings are reproduced in miniature.

Coimbra Environs

Portugal's largest and finest Roman ruins lie 17 km (10 miles) south of Coimbra, at **Conimbriga**, close to the pottery town of Condeixa-a-Nova. Though the extensive site is still being excavated, remnants of fountains, thermal pools, a sophisticated heating system, a large villa, and spectacular colorful mosaics—some of the finest under roofing at the Casa das Fontes—have been unearthed. Conimbriga had become a significant Roman town by 25 BC, though many of the greatest finds here date to the 2nd and 3rd centuries AD. A large museum displays some of the valuable finds from the area.

Along the Mondego, 28 km (17 miles) west of Coimbra, is the sturdy and imposing 14th-century castle at

Montemor-o-Velho (the home town of the wanderer Fernão Mendes Pinto), affording superb views. Here, too, is the fine Manueline church of Santa Maria de Alcáçova, founded in 1090.

One of Portugal's most ancient forests, land that inspires an almost mystical reverence for its citizens, is 25 km (15 miles) north of Coimbra, at **Buçaco**. The forest is home to more than 700 types of trees, and was once the preserve of Benedictine monks—women were not allowed to enter. Footpaths meander all over the thick, tranquil forest, ideal for long walks. Tucked within the forest is the celebrated, fantastically ornate Hotel Palace do Buçaco (see page 175), formerly a royal summer retreat, and a curious stone monastery, the Mosteiro dos Carmelitas. For further relaxation, the nearby town of **Luso** is full of elegant 19th-century buildings, casino, and thermal spas.

The Coast

The prettiest stretch of coast in the south of the Beira Litoral is near the ancient pine forest of the **Pinhal de Leiria**; superb beaches can be found at **São Pedro de Moel** (21 km/13 miles north of Nazaré).

Figueira da Foz, 42 km (26 miles) to the west of Coimbra at the mouth of the Mondego River, has developed from a fishing village into a lively resort popular with the Portuguese. The town beach is large, and separate smaller beaches cater to surfers and families.

Praia de Mira (35 km/22 miles north of Figueira and 6 km/4 miles west of the inland town of Mira) is located by a small lagoon. Characterized by its wooden stilt-houses, it lacks the lively nightlife or accommodations of Figueira (camping is available), though it does have unspoiled and uncrowded beaches and dunes.

The main resort along this stretch of coast is historic **Aveiro**, 52 km (32 miles) to the south of Porto and 29 km (18 miles) north of Mira. Aveiro's unique way of life has developed around its lagoon (Ria). The town was an important port until 1575, when a sandbar formed across the River Vouga, cutting the port off from the sea and creating a vast lagoon. A canal was cut in 1808, and the ria was traversed by Dutch-style canals and bridges. The Municipal Museum, in the old Convento de Jesus, displays religious art, including the massive 18th-century Chapel of Princesa Santa Joana. The tourist office on Rua João Mendonça can arrange boat trips to explore extensive salt pans and see the rich variety of birdlife.

Beira Alta

On the way from Coimbra towards Viseu (87 km/54 miles northeast), the land becomes emphatically rural. Small terraced farms, accompanied by stone houses, donkeys, and grape vines, sit among forested hills. This is the Dão wine region, whose oaky red wines are named after the River Dão, a tributary of the Mondego.

Viseu is a dignified and historic town, supposedly home to Viriathus, the Lusitanian hero who organized the opposition to the Roman invasion of 147 BC. The scenic old town is centered around the Praça da Sé, with its central pillory and wealth of historic buildings. The bulky twin-towered cathedral, originally Romanesque, was redesigned in the 17th century. The classical cloister has Ionic columns on the first level and Doric on the second. The other church on the square, the bright white Igreja Misericórdia, features a terrific baroque façade but an unprepossessing interior.

The top sight in Viseu, and one of Portugal's most important art museums, is the **Museu de Grão Vasco**,) which inhabits the former archbishop's palace next to the cathedral. Vasco Fernandes, more commonly referred to as Grão Vasco (the Great), founded the city's school of painting in the 16th century. Huge, bold panels of his work are on view, including "São Pedro," "Pentecost," and "Assunção da Virgem," as are those of the various Flemish artists who influenced the Viseu School, and those of Vasco's great Portuguese rival, Gaspar Vaz. Perhaps the most interesting exhibit is the 14-panel depiction of the life of Christ, painted by the school of Grão Vasco in 1501–1506 and transferred from the altar of the Viseu cathedral in the 18th century.

The Planalto

Towards the northeast of the Beira Alta is the barren plateau of the **Planalto** ("High Plain"), a wild, cold, and sparsely populated region, but important enough to have been fought over by Portugal and Spain. The plateau's isolation attracted many Jews fleeing the Inquisition. The atmospheric walled town of **Trancoso** (43 km/26 miles to the north of Guarda) records this heritage in the stone carvings above the doorways of Jewish houses. From miles around, you can see the powerful castle walls and strong keep built by Dom Dinis to fortify the border against Spain.

Almeida (65 km/40 miles east) also boasts well-preserved fortifications, a legacy of its position virtually on the Spanish border. The town is enclosed within star-shaped fortifications, reminiscent of those at Elvas in the Alentejo.

Serra da Estrêla

The **Serra da Estrêla**, just southwest of Guarda, offers Portugal's highest mountains, at 1,991 m (6,532 ft), and some fantastic scenery for hiking through the Parque

Natural (Natural Park). **Seia** makes a good base to explore the serra, as does **Penhas da Saúde**, the site of Portugal's only ski resort.

Linhares, which dates to 1169, is one of Portugal's most charming towns. Its moss-covered stone houses and tiny cobbled streets are pre-served museum-like, though it still seems like a real town. Linhares boasts a stretch of Roman road and a scenic medieval castle with splendid views of granite peaks and the Rio Mondego valley. Details of hiking

> **Portugal's famous sheep-milk serra cheese comes from the mountain meadows of the Serra da Estrela. The soft, tangy queijo da serra is served throughout the country.**

routes are available at the tourist office in Guarda or Covilhã, or at the park information offices in Gouveia, Manteigas, or Seia.

Some 20 km (12 miles) from Guarda is tiny **Belmonte**, with a carefully restored 13th-century castle and Jewish Quarter, home to this day to a Jewish community.

Covilhã, a further 20 km (12 miles) south, has become a base for exploring the Serra because of its location close to the highest peaks and the ski fields. This mountainous area produced several explorers who would help form the Portuguese empire: From Covilhã came Pêro de Covilhã, who explored India and Ethiopia in the late 15th century, and born in Belmonte was Pedro Álvares Cabral, who discovered Brazil in 1500.

Beira Baixa

Throughout the Lower Beira, agricultural plains and orchards stretch out between rocky hills and sites of ancient settlements.

The main city in the region is **Castelo Branco**, invaded by the Spanish so often that little of historical interest survives. It is still a pleasant city, with small cobbled alleyways leading up to the ruined "White Castle" at the highest point of the town. The Paço Episcopal (Bishop's Palace) is home to a regional museum, displaying a splendid collection of highly elaborate *colchas* (bedspreads), as well as 16th-century tapestries. The elegant formal Palace Gardens are laid out with an array of baroque statues, sculpted hedges, fountains, and pools. The nearby Miradouro de São Gens affords a good view of the city.

The atmospheric and intensely Portuguese village of **Monsanto,** located about 50 km (31 miles) to the northeast of Castelo Branco, balances on a dramatic rocky outcrop between massive boulders. The streets are too narrow for cars, but a short walk to the castle at the top is worth the effort for the impressive stonework and the view. A beautiful, but roofless, 13th-century Romanesque church can also be seen. A new pousada has just opened here.

THE NORTH

Porto and the Douro Valley

Portugal's prosperous second city, Porto (also written Oporto in English, meaning "the Port"), hugs a gorge at the mouth of the Douro river. The former Roman settlement of Portus, it combined with Calus, its twin town on the opposite bank, to become known as Portucale in the early Middle Ages.

Despite its history and economic importance, Porto is industrious and less self-conscious than Lisbon. Even with splendid bridges crossing the Douro and a red-roofed jumble of buildings creeping up the hillside, its attractions are less obvious than the capital's. Still, many visitors develop a real attraction to the city. Walking is the best way to explore it, despite the many hills that spill down to the river. The city has a new sense of vitality, with a spate of new architecture, art galleries and chic shops and restaurants. Porto was named European Capital of Culture for 2001.

The river that flows all the way to the Spanish border has always been the source of Porto's wealth. The Douro snakes past the terraced vineyards of the Douro Valley. Those vineyards produce fine table wines and, most famously, the rich fortified wine known as port (which took its name from the city). Traditionally port wine was shipped downriver in oak barrels loaded on *barcos rabelos* (flat-bottomed square-sailed boats) to be stored in the cool and damp port lodges (merchants' warehouses) in Vila Nova de Gaia, across the river from Porto. The wines are still stored there, even though they are now transported by truck.

Porto

The city, which began down by the river, has expanded considerably beyond the old walls. **Praça da Liberdade** (Liberty Square) in the upper level now marks the center of the town. Not far from here is the main tourist office, up Avenida dos Aliados and beside the City Hall, at Rua Clube Fenianos 25. For a splendid view over Porto's colorful jumble of streets and crumbling facades, head west out of the Praça, down Rua Clérigos, and climb the church belltower of the imposing Baroque **Igreja de Clérigos**.

A couple of blocks east of the tower (and south of the Praça da Liberdade) is the airy and ornate **Estação de São Bento**, far too handsome to be a mere railway hub. Completed in 1916, its lobby is decorated with wonderful *azulejo* (tile) panels depicting important scenes from the city's history, making it a legitimate tourist attraction.

The serpentine Douro River separates Porto, Portugal's second city, from Gaia.

Just south of the railway station is the Cathedral District. The 12th-century Romanesque **Sé** (Cathedral) is bare and austere—more fortress than church. In the 18th century, an attempt was made to improve its plodding appearance with some baroque additions, but the church remains rather lifeless. Inside the cathedral, a beautiful baroque silver altarpiece is worth a look, as is the rose window. Within these granite walls, João I married his English bride, Philippa of Lancaster, in 1387 (the scene is depicted in azulejos in São Bento railway station), thus sealing the ancient alliance between Portugal and England—an alliance with particular strength in Porto due to the overwhelming English involvement in the port wine trade.

Nearby, the **Casa-Museu Guerra Junqueiro** (Guerra Junqueiro Museum) on Rua de Dom Hugo is the 18th-century home of the Portuguese poet, Guerra Junqueiro. The charming museum displays his furniture and collection of art. The church of **Santa Clara**, a bit east of the cathedral on Largo 1 de Dezembro, remains a bit of a secret and a little difficult to find. Renaissance on the exterior and Rococo within, its exuberantly carved interior is definitely worth seeking out.

The riverside quay, the **Cais da Ribeira**, is an intriguing and slightly grungy area popular with tourists and diners. The old docks hold innumerable seafood restaurants. Tour boats tie up here and offer short river tours, beneath the city's scenic bridges, as well as week-long trips up the Douro to Régua (see page 67). The impressive **Ponte Dom Luís I** (a 172-m bridge built in 1886) looms over the colorful houses of the Ribeira and spans the river to the south bank, where the port lodges (*cavas*) of Vila Nova de Gaia are located (see page 59).

Just uphill from the river is the **Bolsa** district, named after the elegant 19th-century Stock Exchange on the Praça do Infante Dom Henrique. The ornate Neo-Classical building no longer functions as a stock exchange, but guided tours show visitors around the opulent interior. The highlight is the **Salão Árabe** (Arab Room), where the Moorish style of the Alhambra in Granada was lavishly recreated.

Next door is the city's finest church, the **Igreja de São Francisco**, on Rua do Infante D. Henrique. Conventionally Gothic on the outside, the church's interi-

La Vila Nova de Gaia, across the river from Porto, is known for its port lodges.

or is like an explosion in a gold factory. Gilded rococo details swathe the walls from ground to ceiling. The most impressive feature is the "Tree of Jesse," an elaborately carved, gilded and painted 18th-century wood sculpture on the northern wall. The attention-getting piece depicts the family geneaology of Christ. Opposite the church is a small but interesting museum with relics of the old monastery and catacombs.

Also near the Bolsa is the **Casa do Infante**, supposedly the site, if not the actual building, where Henry the Navigator was born (see page 18). This entire block was recently under extensive restoration to become a large city museum. Citizens of Porto are very proud of their association with Henry, especially since their city was where the fleet for the 1415 assault on Ceuta was fitted out. For this patriotic venture against the Moors of North Africa, the

A church tower stands out above Porto's intriguing quayside district of Cais da Ribeira.

The Salão Árabe (Arab Room, above) is the highlight of the Bolsa district's Neo-Classical Stock Exchange building (right), a re-creation of Alhambra that no longer functions for trading, but as a place for visitors to gaze in wonder.

people of Porto surrendered the finest cuts of meat in their stores to the navy and lived on tripe instead, thus earning their honorable nickname of *tripeiros* (literally "tripe eaters," as people from Porto are commonly known).

Some of Porto's other interesting museums are northwest of the town center. The **Museu Soares dos Reis** (on Rua Dom Manuel II) is a wonderful collection of fine art housed in an 18th-century Palácio dos Carrancas. Portuguese artists from the 15th to the 20th centuries are well represented, including paintings by Josefa de Óbidos and sculptures by Soares dos Reis. Look for his *O Desterrado*, a thoughtful work in marble. Also on display are goods that once formed the basis of Portuguese trade with the Orient, especially ceramics.

The **Museu Romântico/Solar do Vinho do Porto** (Romantic Museum and Port Institute), Quinta da Macieirinha, Rua Entre-Quintas 220 (west of Clérigos), displays a collection of 19th-century art and furniture in the last home of the deposed King of Sardinia. Downstairs is the Solar do Vinho do Porto, where you will find hundreds of port vintages waiting to be sampled.

Further removed but well worth seeking out if you have an interest in modern art and architecture, **the Fundação Serralves** (Rua D. João de Castro, 210, about 3 km/2 miles west of Torre de Clérigos) has two primary parts. One is a stark modern shell built by the famed local architect Álvaro Siza Vieira and the other a fabulous pink 1930s Art Deco building, surrounded by lovely gardens and a park populated with goats. Both

A detail from the opulent Salão Árabe in the opulent Stock Exchange on Praça do Infante Dom Henrique.

exhibition spaces house temporary shows by Portuguese and international contemporary artists.

Vila Nova de Gaia

The lower level of the Dom Luís I Bridge leads to the wine cellars of **Vila Nova de Gaia**, which are the low buildings on the southern bank. The familiar and less familiar company names —such as Taylor, Osborne, and Ramos Pinto—appear painted in white and neon signs on the roofs. From the upper level of the bridge is a wonderful view of the cities on both banks.

> **Look for the romantic old tram at the bottom of the hill from the Bolsa. Still in use, it takes workers and tourists back and forth along the waterfront. It will deposit you at the Museu do Carro Eléctrico (Tram Museum), which includes the first tram employed back in 1872.**

Although it is no longer required by law, most port is still blended, stored, and aged in the **port wine lodges** of Gaia (as the riverfront town is commonly called). Almost all were founded after the Treaty of Methuen in 1703, under which the English agreed to reduce the tariffs on port wine imports. Most winemaker companies offer free tours of their lodges, explaining the production process, types of port, and the effects of river floods, and offer visitors a free sample. Whether you tour one of the large-scale international port producers (such as Sandeman) or the smaller, more intimate lodges of Portuguese family-owned firms such as Calém or Fonseca, a visit is a good introduction to the wonders of port.

Coastal Excursions Near Porto

Porto's nearest beaches lie to the west, where the Douro passes a large sandbar and meets the sea at **Foz do Douro**

Although it is no longer required by law, most port is still blended, stored, and aged in the port wine lodges of Gaia.

(Mouth of the Douro). In the 19th century, Foz was a very popular resort, but the water is now heavily polluted. Nevertheless, the beaches and restaurants still make an enjoyable day out, and a scenic old tram (number 18) provides excursions from the resort to the 17th-century Castelo do Queijo (Cheese Castle).

Further north, the beach resorts of the Minho's Costa Verde are at least clean, even if none too warm. The nearest one to Porto is the twin resort area of Vila do Conde/Póvoa de Varzim, 27 km (16 miles) to the north. **Vila do Conde** is the decidedly more pleasant and less developed of the two.

Póvoa do Varzim is a short walk north from Vila do Conde, but is a much livelier and more built-up resort, with a casino. An interesting diversion inland from here is to

Rates, where you can add a dash of culture to the days spent on the beach by looking around the beautiful 11th-century Romanesque church.

The Douro Valley

The Douro Valley extending along the river east toward the Spanish border is one of the most attractive regions in Portugal, sprinkled with small villages, impressive *quintas* (agricultural estates), and beautifully terraced vineyards that dramatically hug the river as it courses through the valley. Cruises run from the Ribeira waterfront in Porto, up to Régua and Pinhão, some lasting a day and others an entire week. Others run between Pinhão all the way to Pocinho, near the border with Spain. Alternatively, you can travel up or down the length of the Douro Valley by train—a spectacular ride

Calém, one of the small family-owned port lodges in Gaia, offers tours of the facilities and samples of the product.

—or meander through the region by car. For additional information, contact the tourist office in Porto.

Upriver from the sandbank at its mouth, the Douro runs between Porto and the port lodges of Vila Nova de Gaia, passing beneath a series of impressive bridges and on towards port-wine territory. The railway line from Porto skips the first 60 km (37 miles) of the river—but this is the least interesting stretch. The line eventually joins the river near **Ribadouro**, proceeding along the northern bank, past small towns and fields where the haystacks, set on cross-shaped supports, look from a distance like scarecrows.

Attractive **Amarante** sits on a gorge of the Tâmega (a tributary of the Douro) and makes a good stop if you are driving along the road from Porto towards Mesã Frio and Régua. Baronial mansions with gaily painted balconies overlooking the river line the streets. Rising above a handsome stone arched bridge and leafy park, the church of the former 16th-century monastery of **São Gonçalo** is well worth a visit, especially if you are looking for love: It hosts a pilgrimage in June for women seeking husbands (with the exchange of phallic-shaped cakes—a remarkably literal step in the mating dance).

The river bends and twists, widens and narrows among green terraced hills. The port trade prompted the growth of **Peso da Régua** (usually called just Régua), 70 km (43 miles) east of Porto. Régua was once the main port used to ship young wines downriver in *barcos rabelos* (flat-bottomed wooden boats) to Vila Nova de Gaia. Though the railways took over for transport from Pinhão (at the confluence of the Douro and Pinhão rivers), and today the wine goes mostly by road, Régua remains an important transportation and commercial hub.

The Secrets of Port Wine—Vinho do Porto

The Douro Valley, which produces the grapes that make port wine, became the world's first demarcated wine-growing region in 1757. Port is now legendary among wines, and one of the best reasons for visiting the Douro Valley is to taste (or even indulge in) a variety of ports—such as vintage ports, aged tawnys, and late bottle vintages—and to get up close and personal with the historic winemaking traditions of Portugal's most famous product. A "Port Wine Route" (Rota do Vinho do Porto) has been created, linking producers and allowing both novices and wine enthusiasts to visit a number of atmospheric quintas (vineyard estates) throughout the valley. It's even possible to stay at one of the numerous quintas, of which virtually all produce their own port (See Accommodations, page 147).

The freezing winters and blisteringly hot summers in the Douro Valley create a unique microclimate that produces intensely flavorful grapes. The inability to recreate these conditions elsewhere is why true port wine only comes from the north of Portugal. During the harvest (vindima) in late September and early October, the land bursts with color and activity, as whole communities gather together for the picking of the grapes. Though most grapes are now crushed by mechanical means, some small vintners still crush them by foot in giant pressing tanks, in a jubilant atmosphere accompanied by singing and guitar music (and of course, drinking).

Port is a fortified wine; winemakers long ago added grape brandy to stabilize the wines during their long journeys overseas and discovered that the brandy halted fermentation and produced a fresh sweet flavor that deepened as the wine aged.

A vintage is declared only in years of outstanding harvests. Ruby port is a deep red and fruity variety, while tawny is a lighter, more golden color with a nuttier taste. Aged tawnys are blends aged in oak barrels. One type of port not well known outside Portugal is white port (porto branco), made with white grapes and served as an aperitif. All other varieties are dessert wines, consumed at the end of the meal.

What the town lacks in beauty it makes up for in industry. The headquarters of port winemakers, **Casa do Douro**, remains in Régua (visitors can pick up a map of the Port Wine Route there). Sandeman operates a large modern winery just across the river, and Cockburns is up the hill overlooking Régua.

Mesão Frio, 12 km (7 miles) west of Régua, is the gateway to the Douro. Sitting high above the river, amidst the rambling hills of the Serra do Marão, it is an excellent place to relax. There are a number of beautiful *solares* (manor houses), some of which offer accommodations.

The prettiest town in the area is the affluent center of **Lamego**, south of the Douro, 13 km (8 miles) from Régua. Although technically part of the Beiras region, Lamego's soul belongs to the Douro. As well as growing grapes for port, Lamego also produces a fine champagne-like wine called Raposeira. Lamego was once a pilgrimage center, a heritage reflected in one of Portugal's most famous churches, Baroque **Nossa Senhora dos Remédios** and the stunning stone staircase that climbs the hill. Inspired by another shrine, Bom Jesus (see page 76) near Braga, the monumental staircase is lined with statues, azulejos, fountains, and chapels. Some penitents still heroically climb the 600-plus steps on their knees, especially during the great annual pilgrimage on 8 September.

Lamego has a wealth of handsome Baroque mansions, as well as a scenic 13th-century castle and a 16th-century Sé (cathedral) with a 12th-century tower. The **Museu de Lamego** in the old bishop's palace houses a fine collection of Flemish tapestries and religious statues, as well as paintings by Grão Vasco of the Viseu school (see page 56).

Pinhão, upriver from Régua (both the train trip and drive along the river in this stretch are stunning), is an enjoyable little town with deep connections to the port wine trade. The tiny train station displays azulejos depicting the harvest, and many important quintas owned by the biggest port concerns, as well as independently owned vineyards, hug the hills near here. Taylor, one of the major wine players, recently opened an excellent hotel in Pinhão, the appropriately named Vintage House.

From Pinhão to Pocinho, the train snakes along the Douro's switchbacks with stunning views at every turn (2 hours roundtrip). Another good route is north to Tua. If you want to get closer to the wine production, you'll need to have a car or arrange a tour with one of the quintas or local hotels. Other towns ensconced in the craggy green hills and pretty terraced vineyards are Alijó, São João da Pesqueira, and Sabrosa.

Having little to do with wine, but plenty to do with the historic underpinnings of this region, are the archaeological park and sublime Paleolithic rock drawings near **Vila Nova de Foz Côa** (8 km/5 miles south of Pocinho). Discovered only in 1992, the engravings of deer, goats, and horses constitute the largest outdoor assembly of **Paleolithic rock art** in Europe. Visits are by guided tour only, through the headquarters of the foundation overseeing the project. Attendance is strictly limited, and slots to visit the three sites are often reserved weeks in advance. Visit the Web site of **Parque Arqueológico do Côa** <www.ipa.min-cultura.pt/coa> to arrange visits in advance, or stop by the headquarters in Vila Nova de Foz Côa (Av. Gago Coutinho, 19 A; Tel. 351/279 768 260/1). Visits last a couple of hours (to each site, arranged separately) and transportation to the sites is included.

THE MINHO

The lush northwestern province of the Minho north of Porto is one of the most beautiful regions of Portugal. The intensely green area is renowned for its mountains and forests, *vinho verde* ("green wine"), and Costa Verde ("Green Coast").

Portugal originated in this corner just below Galicia, the one-time Celtic settlement in Spain. It was recaptured from the Moors early in the Christian Reconquest campaign and, when Afonso Henriques declared himself the first king in 1139, the Minho became the independent state of Portucale (covering an area from the Douro to the River Minho). Numerous splendid monuments survive in two beautiful historic cities, Guimarães and Braga. The region is reputed to be one of the most religious and conservative in Portugal.

Guimarães

 A large sign in the center of **Guimarães** (49 km/30 miles northeast of Porto) declares "Aqui Nasceu Portugal" ("Here was born Portugal"), testament to the historic nature of this medieval gem of a small city.

The city's compact yet sturdy 10th-century castle seems to have grown out of the rocky hillock. Seven towers protect a large central keep lined with unusual triangular battlements that look like serrated teeth. Afonso Henriques, the first King of Portugal, is said to have been born in the castle and baptized nearby, in the small Romanesque **Igreja de São Miguel do Castelo.**

Just down the hill is the massive **Paço dos Duques de Bragança** (Ducal Palace), a mix between a French château and a crusader castle. Once the home of the Dukes of Bragança, it fell into disrepair and was reconstructed from ruin in the 1930s. Though the reconstruction is not historically accurate, a 45-minute tour of the interior is interesting for the large collection of antiques.

The historic city center runs down the hill from the castle along the Rua de Santa Maria to a series of beautiful medieval squares surrounded by old townhouses. The triangular **Largo de Santiago** is flanked by the arcaded 14th-century Old Town Hall and a series of townhouses converted into the Pousada da Oliveira inn.

Through the arcades is the central **Largo da Oliveira**, where the excellent **Museu Alberto Sampaio** is located in Nossa Senhora da Oliveira (the Collegiate Church of Our Lady of the Olive Tree). The museum houses stone carvings from the convent in a 13th-century cloister, as well as gold, ceramics, and religious items. There is also a room devoted to the battle of Aljubarrota (see page 17); exhibits include the shirt worn by João I during the fray.

The other notable museum in Guimarães is the **Museu de Martins Sarmento**, named for the 19th-century excavator of the Citânia de Briteiros, an ancient settlement of Celto-Iberians. Artifacts displayed, recovered from Briteiros and other sites, include carved stone lintels, tools, and several fascinating sculptures, such as the enormous pre-Roman Colossus of Pedralva.

In the Penha Hills above the city is the lovely **Mosteiro de Santa Marinha da Costa,** founded in the 12th century. This lovely former monastery has been remarkably restored to form one of Portugal's most evocative pousadas. The views of Guimarães down the hill are outstanding. The most enjoyable way up to Penha, which is 5 km (3 miles) by road, is to take the fast *teleférico* (cable car). Catch it at the end of Rua de Doutor José Sampaio.

Near Guimarães

Just 15 km (9 miles) from Guimarães on the way to Braga is the prehistoric site of **Briteiros**, set on a rocky hillside overlooking a series of valleys and forested hills. Inhabited by Celt-Iberians from around the 4th century BC to the 4th century AD, the entire hillside is covered with the remains of the best-preserved *citânia* (Celtic hill settlement) in Portugal. The walls of more than a hundred circular houses are visible — two have been rebuilt to give an idea of what the settlement once looked like — in addition to roads, drainage channels, and a defensive wall. A hike downhill leads to a mysterious structure that has been interpreted both as a burial chamber and as a bath house (it now appears to be the latter). The most impressive artifacts from the site can be viewed in the Martins Sarmento Museum in Guimarães.

Braga

Gracious and bustling **Braga** (22 km/13 miles northwest of Guimarães) is the 12th-century ecclesiastical center of Portugal, today famous for its Holy Week celebrations (see page 136). It has more than 30 churches to bolster its religious reputation. The old town, which is peppered with several fine turn-of-the-century cafés on or near Praça República (including Café Astoria and A Brasileira), is a delight to wander around.

The original Romanesque exterior of the **Sé** (Cathedral) has been embellished over the years in a number of styles. Inside are two extravagant golden organs, replete with trumpets, a carved choir of Brazil wood, and a painted ceiling flanking the nave near the entrance. The true wealth of the Archbishopric of Braga, though, can be glimpsed in the cathedral's stunning but somewhat disheveled **Museu de Arte Sacra** (Museum of Religious Art), crammed with gold and silver pieces, including the cross that Cabral took on his pioneering voyage to Brazil in 1500, polychromatic figures, and azulejos. Across a courtyard are a couple of 14th-century chapels, one with a tomb of the parents of the first King of Portugal and the other a mummified archbishop who died in 1397.

The pedestrian-only Rua do Souto runs right through the middle of town, passing the square of the former **Archbishop's Palace**, nowadays a library, and an old medieval keep. Before reaching the center at the Praça da Republica, you will find the tourist office, housed in a marvelous art deco building.

Braga is known for its churches, but it has many splendid Baroque mansions as well. Just west of city center is **Palacio dos Biscainhos**, built in the 17th century (the decoration is 18th-century). The house reflects the refined lifestyle enjoyed by the nobility, with *azulejo* panels showing falconry, displays of Chinese porcelain, and delightful

The Citania de Briteiros, near Guimarães, is the best-preserved Celtic hill settlement in Portugal.

gardens. South of Praça da República, the magnificently blue-tiled **Casa do Raio**, known as the Casa do Mexicano, is now a hospital.

Beyond Braga is one of the north's most frequently photographed sights, the 18th-century pilgrimage church of **Bom Jesus do Monte**, situated in the mountains 4 km (2 miles) east of Braga. The twin-towered Baroque church is principally notable for the grand staircase that leads up to it. It is lined with chapels featuring the 14 Stations of the Cross, lichen-covered statues, urns, and fountains. The devout climb all the way up on their knees; the less committed can walk or take the funicular railway and stay in one of the three hotels located at the top.

Barcelos

West of Braga toward the coast is **Barcelos**, home of the country's largest agricultural fair (held every Thursday in the massive open square, the Campo da República). Every kind of animal and myriad produce from the Minho is on sale, as well as the famous pottery and handicrafts of Barcelos.

In one corner of the square is the beautiful church of **Nossa Senhor Bom Jesus**

Freshly cut bacalhau on sale at the weekly Barcelos fair.

da Cruz, an octagonal baroque building. The old part of town continues on down to the River Cávado. The Palace of the Counts of Barcelos overlooks the river, but was abandoned after the 1755 earthquake. Its shell now houses the various stone artifacts making up the **Museu Arqueológico**.

The Minho Coast

The Minho's **Costa Verde** (Green Coast) is low-key compared with the crowded beaches of the Algarve. Beautiful beaches run in a virtually unbroken sweep from Porto all the way up to the Galician (Spanish) border on the River Minho. The

Make a Baroque pilgrimage to Bom Jesus do Monte.

region isn't overly touristed, though; it isn't unusual to see oxen pulling carts piled high with seaweed for fertilizer.

The only major resort along this coastline is the splendid city of **Viana do Castelo** (60 km/38 miles north of Porto), which is much more than just beaches. Viana is bounded by the estuary of the River Lima to the south and by the wooded Monte de Santa Luzia to the north. The triangular Praça da República forms the center of the historic old town, around which are a series of *palácios* constructed during Viana's heyday in the 15th century as a *bacalhau* fishing center. Especially interesting are the fine

16th-century Renaissance Misericórdia (Almshouse) and Gothic Igreja Matriz.

Rising above Viana is the scenic **Monte de Santa Luzia**. Like Bom Jesus, it has a pilgrimage church on the summit and a funicular railway, though no grand staircase. Though the church itself isn't remarkable, the views from the plaza in front take in the north and south coast, the River Lima, and Viana itself. There is also a fine hotel (see page 177) and an excavated *citânia* (pre-Roman hillfort) faintly reminiscent of Briteiros (see page 73).

Viana's main beach lies to the south, across the estuary at **Praia do Cabedelo**, accessible by ferry or road bridge. Heading north along the coast from Viana there is little sand, but the rocks are popular for fishing. The small, quaint resort town of **Vila Praia de Âncora** is 16 km (10 miles) further up the coast.

The River Lima

Inland from Viana do Castelo, the beautiful flat Lima Valley runs east through a gentle agricultural landscape dotted with haystacks. The Romans settled this attractive area and built a bridge at **Ponte de Lima**, 23 km (14 miles) upstream from Viana. A Roman bridge (*ponte*) still

Boats troll leisurely along the waterways of Porto and Minho Valley.

spans the Lima, though the town is perhaps better known for its ancient bi-monthly market. The hills on the north side offer scenic walks, and Ponte de Lima has an excellent choice of accommodations in old manor houses, part of the Turismo de Habitação plan (see ACCOMMODATION, page 147).

Ponte de Barca (18 km/11 miles further east along the Lima) is also an appealing town. Home to a fine 15th-century bridge, it also hosts a bi-monthly market by the river. The town serves as a good base for some pleasant hill walks, past small, unspoiled Minho villages.

The Peneda-Gerês National Park

The Lima Valley continues east towards the river's source in Spain, passing through the wild and wonderful **Peneda-Gerês National Park**. The park is one of the most visited parts of the Minho, yet it is very easy to hike up into the mountains and find yourself alone with the mountain goats. The park boasts mountains, river valleys, megalithic monuments (*antas*), waterfalls, and small mountain hamlets. Fifteen species of wild flowers are unique to the park. Numerous tracks crisscross the area, passing reservoirs that are perfect for a dip after a long day's hike.

The park is divided into two parts: the much-visited Serra do Gerês, and the quieter, wilder Serra da Peneda to the north. **Caldas do Gerês** is the principal tourist base, a slightly tattered spa town. Hiking advice is available from the park information office, and the tourist office can provide details of local accommodations and outdoor activities, such as horse trekking. The nearby Miradouro do Gerês has a splendid view over much of the park.

The best approach to the northern Peneda section of the park is from either Monção or Melgaço, on the River

Minho. The main point of access for the eastern part of the park is Caldas do Gerês, but there is another fascinating route starting from Chaves (see page 83), in Trás-os-Montes, that crosses a truly remote area passing by the gigantic **Pisões dam**.

The River Minho

The River Minho forms the northern border between the Minho (Portugal) and Galicia (Spain). Its banks are lined by numerous beautiful walled towns and powerful fortresses. The charming town of **Vila Nova de Cerveira**, about 20 km (12 miles) northeast from the coastal resort of Vila Praia de Âncora, is typical of them, with thick town walls and a regular ferry service across the river to Spain. Inside the walls of the old fortress is a luxurious pousada.

Farther upriver, **Valença do Minho** boasts dramatic and powerful defensive walls (also housing a pousada). Within is a well-preserved town of winding streets and quaint 17th-century buildings.

TRÁS-OS-MONTES

The name given Trás-os-Montes—literally, "Beyond the Mountains"—suggests how remote, and even forgotten, it is, even in this small country. Portugal's poorest region is one of deep river valleys separated by rocky hilltops and dense forests. The region retains a sleepy medieval air. Some modernization is occurring thanks to development funds from the European Union and the influence of returning migrants, but the countryside is still dominated by a traditional agricultural and peasant way of life.

The land is divided by temperature: the northern part, Terra Fria ("Cold Land"), experiences very harsh winters, while Terra Quente ("Hot Land") is more temperate,

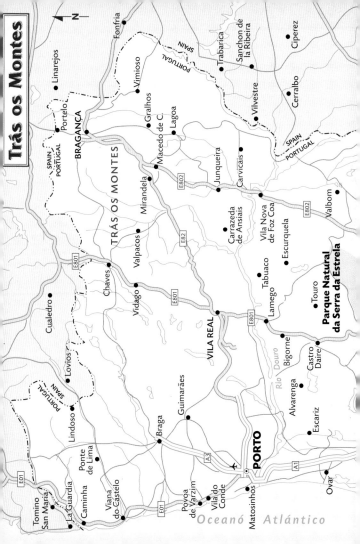

containing large vineyards in the Upper Douro Valley. The white almond blossoms in spring are one of the most sublime sights in Portugal.

The region's overpowering isolation is very evident on curvy backroads, where drivers must contend with men straggling along the side with hoes hoisted over their shoulders, women carrying bunches of branches, and serious-looking farmers towing donkey-led carts.

Vila Real and the Southwest

Vila Real is the largest town in the region, with a population of 30,000. Mostly modern and industrial, it sits on the edge of the impressive deep gorge of the River Corgo, a tributary of the Douro. A scenic way of reaching Vila Real is as a passenger on the narrow-gauge train from Peso da Régua (see page 68) in the Douro Valley. Vila Real itself is somewhat less than fascinating, but it's surrounded by several interesting sights nearby, and the Alvão and Marão mountain ranges rise abruptly just outside town, making this an excellent base for hiking and climbing.

At the center of the town is the broad Avenida Carvalho Araújo, where you will find the cathedral and the tourist office in an old mansion. If you continue south, you will pass the 14th-century **Capela de São Bras** and be rewarded by a fine view of the gorge.

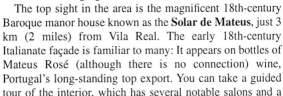
The top sight in the area is the magnificent 18th-century Baroque manor house known as the **Solar de Mateus**, just 3 km (2 miles) from Vila Real. The early 18th-century Italianate façade is familiar to many: It appears on bottles of Mateus Rosé (although there is no connection) wine, Portugal's long-standing top export. You can take a guided tour of the interior, which has several notable salons and a

well-stocked library, but the exterior and formal gardens are the standout features.

Chaves and Environs

Beyond Vila Real, Trás-os-Montes becomes noticeably wilder. The main road to Chaves follows a scenic route along the valley of the Corgo. **Vidago** is an elegant 19th-century spa town, 17 km (11 miles) before Chaves, boasting the Edwardian Palace Hotel, gardens, and a nine-hole golf course. The spa is only open in summer.

Chaves, a mere 12 km (7 miles) from Spain, is a quiet place—at least now that it isn't suffering repeated attacks from the invading Spanish. The last military attack took place in 1912, but waves of Spanish shoppers still invade the town every weekend in search of bargain prices on a number of goods. The town's strategic role as a border-crossing is reflected in its name (Chaves means "Keys") and by its two 17th-century fortresses (the Forte de São Francisco has been converted into a superior hotel). There is also a 14th-century keep, which today houses an interesting Military Museum.

Chaves was an important Roman spa town, known as Aquae Flaviae, and its hot springs (good for rheumatism and gout) remain open in summer. The Romans also built a bridge over the River Tâmega, which is still in use and retains its ancient milestone. You can learn more about the town's Roman past in the **Museu da Região Flaviense** (Regional Museum) on Praça Camões. The attractive, well-maintained old town also has several interesting medieval squares and two fine churches.

Long before the Romans arrived, the region's prehistoric inhabitants left a series of carvings on a massive granite boulder at **Outeiro Machado**, 3 km (2 miles) outside

Chaves. The carved symbols are believed to have been associated with rituals involving sacrifice—easy to believe in this otherworldly setting.

Bragança and the Northeast

The route from Chaves to Bragança is particularly attractive: the road winds over mountain passes, through pine forests, and past the spines of bare, rocky hillsides. The new and partially completed homes of returned emigrants stand out from the simple houses strung alongside fields still worked by donkey plow.

Bragança is a remote outpost, but one with a grand history. It was here that Catherine of Bragança, the wife of the English king, Charles II, was born. She took with her to England the custom of drinking afternoon tea, and control of Bombay, thus beginning England's interest in India. Catherine's family served as rulers of Portugal between 1640 and 1910, but they preferred their estate at Vila Viçosa in the Alentejo (see page 95) to this lonely vastness.

The town is dominated by its **Citadel** (Cidadela), one of the best-known in Portugal, and by the bleak surrounding hills. The fortress encloses a small, medieval village of white-washed houses where tourists still raise eyebrows. The central keep sits on the highest ground and houses an interesting **Museu Militar**, tracing the course of Portuguese military concerns from prehistoric times right through to the colonial wars of the 1970s. In front of the keep is Portugal's most curious *pelourinho*, which stands on top of a primitive granite boar (*porca*), carved in prehistoric times.

Also within the castle is **Igreja de Santa Maria**, with its wavy entrance columns and a lovely painted ceiling. Next door stands a rare example of a 12th-century **Meeting House** (Domus Municipalis), the only surviving Romanesque civic building in Portugal. It has five sides, and the upper floor, decorated with Romanesque arches under a timber roof, was used for assemblies, while the lower floor served as a water cistern.

In the lower town, the unusual **Museu Regional Abade de Baçal** is located in the former Bishop's Palace. The abbot was quite a collector; on display are an eclectic mix of local archaeological finds, clerical items, regional paintings, and costumes. Two churches worth a look are the Renaissance **Igreja de São Bento**, with its contrasting ceiling, part Moorish carved wood and part *trompe l'oeil*; and the **Igreja de São Vicente**, where Pedro I claimed to have married Inês de Castro (see page 45).

The barren and wild **Parque Natural de Montesinho** lies between Bragança and Spain, and is home to a number of small, isolated villages that have striven to keep up their traditions of communal ownership and pre-Christian ritual. They share this landscape with wolves and boars. For hardcore hikers, Montesinho is a delight. For details of campsites, visit the park office in Bragança. The tiny village of **Rio de Onor**, 24 km (15 miles) to the northeast, is a village that time forgot and a geographical oddity. The town straddles the border: half is in Portugal, half in Spain (where it's called Rihonor de Castilla). Locals have long gone back and forth between Portuguese and Spanish, with intermarriage between the two nationalities common.

Miranda do Douro

About as far east as you can get in Trás-os-Montes, **Miranda do Douro** stands poised at the edge of the great gorge of the Alto Douro (Upper Douro). Halfway across the modern dam, Spain begins.

Miranda itself is officially a "city," even though it has only some 2,000 inhabitants. Their low white-washed houses and cobbled streets were long ago enclosed by walls to keep the Spanish out—a purpose that failed in 1762, when a force of French and Spanish troops blew up the castle, leaving it a fairly uninspiring ruin.

The event led Miranda to lose its bishop, who decamped to the safety of Bragança. The cold, dark and austere 16th-century **Sé** (cathedral) remains. In the right-hand transept, in a glass case, is a curiosity, a small statue of a boy known as the Menino Jesus da Cartolina. Sporting hand-tailored clothes of a tiny dandy (complete with top hat and several sets of Baby Liberace doll clothes at the ready) the little figure commemorates a 16th-century boy-hero who is said to have saved the city from the Spanish. Locals believed he was Jesus in disguise.

On Largo Dom João III, at the center of the town, is the excellent **Museu da Terra de Miranda**, displaying a selection of traditional Mirandês costumes, ancient ritualistic figures, furniture, and folklore objects. Miranda has its own culture and a distinctive dialect, Mirandês, that freely combines Latin, Portuguese, Spanish, and even some Hebrew. The town is also renowned for its festivals and unique sword dancers, called the *pauliteiros*.

The **gorge** itself is about 2 km (1 mile) away, down a twisting road. The rocky hillsides on both sides of the dam are home to some 80 species of birds, as well as flocks of sheep. Cruise boats on the dammed side of the gorge take trips upriver. On the other side of the dam, the river snakes its way through port-wine country down to Porto.

Central and Southeastern Trás-os-Montes

Mirandela is a pleasant town at the hub of the region's road system, 54 km (33 miles) southeast of Chaves, 64 km (40 miles) southwest of Bragança, and 70 km (43 miles) north-

Next to the Temple is the elegant **Pousada dos Lóios** (see page 178), a state-owned inn that was formerly a convent. Abutting the pousada is the privately owned church of **São João Evangelista** (also known as Lóios, the old church of the same convent). Inside are some of the country's finest examples of *azulejo* tilework, created in the 18th century by the celebrated artist Antônio Oliveira Bernardes and depicting the life of São Lourenço (St. Lawrence). The church holds several other surprises. Hidden beneath trapdoors on either side of the aisle are a Moorish cistern 15 m (50 ft) deep and a collection of monks' bones in the ossuary. There are also confession holes that open onto the pousada's cloister, from where you can spy on diners.

More bones than you can shake a stick at—the startling Chapel of Bones, built from the bones of 5000 monks.

The nearby **Sé** (Cathedral), begun in 1186, betrays its crusading origins with its fortress-like Romanesque style. Note the statues of the Twelve Apostles by the door and their odd gargoyle friends. The impressive eastern wing was rebuilt by Friedrich Ludwig, the architect of the Convent at Mafra (see page 42), using the multicolored marble of the Alentejo. The cathedral has an especially beautiful Gothic cloister and Sacred Art Museum, with an extraordinary impressive collection of relics and clerical vestments. The upper choir is exquisitely carved, with a great Renaissance organ dating to 1562—one of the oldest in Europe.

The **Igreja de São Fransisco** holds one of Évora's greatest (and most macabre) attractions, the **Capela dos Ossos** (Chapel of Bones). The chapel is a large room wholly constructed with the bones of 5,000 monks; skulls form the window frames and femurs cover the columns. Over the entrance is a spooky sign that reminds visitors of their own mortality: *"Nós ossos que aqui estamos, Pelos vossos esperamos"* ("We bones that are here, await the arrival of yours").

The **Museu de Évora**, not far from the cathedral, is housed in the old archbishop's palace. It has an important collection of paintings by the Flemish-inspired "Portuguese School," the finest being a polyptych of 13 panels depicting the *Life of the Virgin* from the early 15th–late 16th century. The altarpiece was removed from the Sé in 1717. The museum also contains an eclectic mix of stone sculptures, including some Roman tombstones, several Arab votive inscriptions, and medieval tomb carvings.

There are several other churches and houses of interest, as well as the old university, but beyond its admirable register of historical monuments, Évora remains a thoroughly charming small city to stroll and take in at a leisurely pace. Rua 5 de Outubro, a long thoroughfare leading to Praça do

Giraldo, is the main shopping street.

Rest of the Alentejo

The fine white-washed town of **Arraiolos**, 21 km (13 miles) north of Évora, is famed for its carpet workshops. The town's handwoven **wool rugs**, in the Moorish-Persian style, have been made here since the 17th century. While they aren't cheap (though cheaper here than elsewhere), they are extremely beautiful.

Another excellent day trip from Évora is to the **megaliths** near **Reguengos de Monsaraz** (36 km/22 miles to the southeast). These baffling prehistoric monuments, or dolmens, consist of standing stones (menhirs) and stone circles

A painted doorway brightens the street in the aging agricultural city of Beja.

(cromlechs) that look like spin-offs from Stonehenge (ask the tourist office in Évora for a pamphlet on these and other dolmens in the area as well as for precise directions).

Near the Spanish border is **Monsaraz**, a quietly stunning fortified hilltop village with cobbled streets and spectacular views over the plains. The castle (now occasionally hosting bullfights) is one in the long chain of fortifications built by Dom Dinis in the 14th century.

The Marble Towns

About 46 km (28 miles) northeast of Évora, marble sup-
plants more mundane building materials for churches and
palaces, thanks to the great number of quarries found at
Estremoz, Borba, and Vila Viçosa.

The largest of these quarries is near **Estremoz**, a walled
town full of gleaming white marble stretching above the
plains. The **Rossio** (Praça Marquês de Pombal) forms the
heart of the lower town and is home to the hustle and bustle of a Saturday market, one of the region's liveliest,
where you can buy the famous pottery of Estremoz, tasty
local cheese, and any of the other agricultural products of
the Alentejo. There is a tourist office on the square, as well
as an interesting **Museu Rural** (Rural Museum) displaying a wealth of idiosyncratic local gadgets and pottery.
Also here is the beautiful marble-faced Câmara Municipal
(Town Hall), converted from an old convent, with impressive *azulejo* panels.

The upper town is reached through medieval walls. Lording
over the town is the 13th-century **Torre das Três Coroas** (castle keep, or Tower of Three Crowns), visible for miles around.
Inside is the *azulejo*-covered chapel of Rainha Santa Isabel,
dedicated to the memo-
ry of Dom Dinis's
sainted queen. To one
side is the white-mar-
ble Royal Palace, now
one of the country's
finest and most in-
demand *pousadas*.

Borba, on the road
to Elvas and Spain, is

The origins of Portugal's megaliths
near Évora have been dated by
archaeologists between the 5th and
3rd centuries b.c. Though their
exact purposes remain unknown,
many experts have asserted that
dolmens served as burial chambers
and demarcated territories. At least
125 megalithic monuments have
been found in the Alentejo region.

more down-to-earth, though its marble buildings betray the source of the local wealth: The people of Borba make their living from extracting marble from quarries, as well as producing fine red and white wines. Every November the town hosts a gregarious wine festival.

Just up the road, 6 km (4 miles) away, is a third marble town, **Vila Viçosa**. The pretty town is most remarkable for its impressive 16th-century **Paço Ducal** (Ducal Palace) of the Bragança family, the last of Portugal's royal dynasties. The Paço used to be the favorite country house of the family, who often preferred hunting in the enormous surrounding park to the fuss of Lisbon or the cold of their palace in Bragança in northern Portugal (see page 84). The guided tour (in Portuguese only) provides an intimate glimpse of the royal apartments as they would have appeared before the assassination of Carlos I in 1908. Next door to the palace is the pousada, in a gorgeously restored 16th-century convent.

Further east, and nearer to Spain, is the mighty frontier fortress town of **Elvas**. The castle walls—among the best-preserved in Portugal—were modernized in the 17th century and given the characteristic star shape that distinguishes the work of Vauban, the French military architect. From the ramparts are superb views of the Portuguese plains and Spain across the border. Nearby is the oldest section of town, with steep cobblestoned streets and hanging laundry. Extending from the city's walls is the **Aqueduto da Amoreira**, an aqueduct some 7 km (4 miles) long that took 124 years to complete. The town's largest church, on Praça da República, is the richly painted **Nossa Senhora da Assunção,** with an elaborate Manueline portal and belltower overlooking the square. **Nossa Senhora dos Aflitos,** another church closer to the castle, has an octagonal shape that reflects the influence of the architecture of the Knights Templar, and the remarkable dome is covered in beautiful 17th-century azulejos.

Northeastern Alentejo

Portalegre is the prosperous, no-nonsense capital of the northern Alentejo, located near the hills and neolithic monuments of the Serra de São Mamede, 59 km (36 miles) north of Estremoz. Its past wealth, based on carpet and silk production, accounts for the graceful 18th-century mansions lining the Rua 19 de Junho. By far the most interesting sight in town, though, is the **Fábrica Real de Tapeçarias** (Tapestry Factory), housed in a 17th-century Jesuit school, where dozens of women use great handlooms to weave carpets from thousands of different shades of wool.

Horse fans should be sure to visit **Alter do Chão** (33 km/20 miles southeast of Portalegre), the location of the Coudelaria de Alter Real (Royal Stud Farm), where Portugal's finest horses are bred. If you arrive in the morning you can watch the Lusitanian and Alter do Chão horses being fed. There is also an interesting museum, and the town has a fine restored castle.

Flôr da Rosa and **Crato** are two small agricultural towns west of Portalegre. In the former is one of the best examples of how the state pousada chain is adapting modern architecture to historic buildings. The inn now occupying the 14th-century **Convento de Flôr da Rosa** is extraordinary. Outside of town, on the road to Aldeia da Mata, is one of the best-preserved **dolmens** in Portugal, a mysterious prehistoric chamber sitting unobtrusively in rolling pastoral lands. In Crato is a stately square with an interesting **Varanda do Grão Prior,** with stone arches under a terrace once used for outdoor Mass, and a municipal museum of local handicrafts and artifacts two doors down. Above town are the curious ruins of the castle, now undergoing extensive restoration.

North of Portalegre is the pleasant town **Castelo de Vide**, whose 14th-century castle is surrounded by gleaming houses that nuzzle against the steeply sloping hill. Further down the hill, the winding alleyways of the **Judiaria** (Jewish Quarter) have survived and make a great place for wandering. Among these houses is the country's oldest surviving synagogue (dating from the 13th century). For centuries the fresh springs at **Fonte de Vila**, close to the handsome main square, the Praça Dom Pedro V, have been another of Castelo de Vide's many attractions.

A steep winding road leads to the dramatically situated medieval walled village **Marvão**. Perched on an outcrop overlooking Spain, the easygoing town is the highest in Portugal (at 862 m/2,800 ft). The 13th-century castle walls appear woven right into the natural rock; the views from atop the ramparts, of both the white-washed town and surrounding area, are stunning. It's not hard to understand why the fortress proved virtually impenetrable. Marvão has almost all the charm of Óbidos (see page 43), but without the slickness or tour bus crowds. Just outside the castle entrance is a handsome **Museu Municipal**, with nice archaeological finds, religious artifacts and altarpieces, and regional costumes.

Baixo (Lower) Alentejo

Of Roman origin (it was a regional capital under Julius Caesar), the agricultural city of **Beja** (78 km/48 miles south of Évora) is at the hub of roads that lead to Lisbon, the Algarve, and across the Alentejo. The old town is particularly attractive.

The decoratively crenellated **Torre de Menagem** in the castle dates to the 13th century and provides a good lookout over the extensive wheatfields of the region. The city's most interesting sight is the **Convento de Nossa Senhora da Conceição**, with its fine Manueline carving, bright Moorish-style azulejos, splendid Baroque chapel, and an explosion of rococo gold leaf. The former convent houses an interesting regional museum with a good archaeological and painting collection. There is also a unique **Museu Visigótico** (Visigothic Art Museum) in Santo Amaro, Beja's oldest church. The new Pousada de São Fransisco has been admirably converted from another convent, once derelict.

The charming, sleepy town of **Serpa** rises neatly above the plains, 30 km (18 miles) east of Beja, on the route to Spain. Beyond the formidable Porta da Beja, a monumental gate in the city wall, small streets wend among bright white houses. Many of the buildings hide small cheese factories, which produce Serpa's famous ewe's milk cheese. The town's castle was partially destroyed by a Spanish attack in 1707, but still affords enjoyable views. The walls continue past a privately owned 17th-century mansion and on to a slender aqueduct, which ends in an ancient well with a working chain-pulley system for drawing water. A small ethnographic museum displays the wares of the agricultural and industrial workers of the area.

From Serpa a rewarding drive takes you south toward the eastern Algarve, through a hilly and sparsely populated landscape where shepherds tend their flocks. Along the way is **Mértola**, an ancient white-washed town founded by the Phoenicians, built up by the Romans, and later seized by the Moors. Perched on a ridge at the junction of the River

The region of Alentejo is known for its stark landscapes and sleepy towns, all resonating with a sense of history.

Guadiana and the smaller Oeiras, the town is protected by Moorish walls and topped by a rather dilapidated castle with a profusion of storks' nests.

Mértola bursts with history: Its church, the Igreja Matriz, betrays a previous incarnation as a mosque with a prayer niche (*mihrab*), while the town hall (now a museum) is constructed on Roman foundations. The Guadiana River continues as far as the Algarve, forming part of the border with Spain. The road that follows its banks is one of the most beautiful access routes between the Alentejo and the Algarve.

Coastal Alentejo

The Alentejo coast, a popular holiday destination with the Portuguese, has a character slightly different from that of the even more popular Algarve. The water here is colder, and the winds and waves greater, but it is also noticeably quieter, more relaxed, and less expensive. Often the best beaches are those near a river estuary, thus giving visitors the choice of surfing in the Atlantic or swimming in the calmer waters of the river.

The northernmost point of the coastal Alentejo is the narrow, sandy peninsula of **Tróia**, 46 km (28 miles) northwest of the attractive town of Alcácer do Sal. Tróia has beaches on both the Sado estuary and the ocean, but the town has been heavily developed in recent years to accommodate ferries from Setúbal (see page 41). Even so, it is worth visiting the remains of the Roman fishing village of Cetobriga. You can escape the crowds on the beaches of the ocean side.

Further to the south and slightly inland is the town of **Santiago do Cacém**, hemmed in by low-lying hills on three sides and crowned by a hilltop castle, which holds a macabre cemetery full of disinterred bones. Scattered about the surrounding hills is a profusion of windmill towers which, without their white canvas sails, look for all the world like ancient cannons. The lagoons of **Santo André** and **Melides** are both easily accessible from Santiago do Cacém and boast long stretches of beach, ocean, and lagoon swimming, and small beachside communities.

THE ALGARVE

To many international visitors, the Algarve *is* Portugal, but the Portuguese see the Algarve as a distinct anomaly. The area's distinctive character owes much to its strong Moorish heritage and its Mediterranean climate, so different from most other parts of the country.

The region's popularity with millions of vacationers has produced an explosion of purpose-built holiday villages. The Algarve is blessed with a number of spectacular beaches, a wonderfully sunny climate, many excellent sporting facilities, and even a handful of quiet and untouristed areas.

Access from one part of the Algarve to another is along the EN125 road, which runs most of the length of the coast. The section of coast stretching from Faro eastwards to Spain, known as the Sotavento Coast, is made up of salt marshes and lagoons, with beautiful sandy beaches on the barrier islands just offshore. The most intensively developed part stretches westward from Faro to Portimão. Here the long beaches are all backed by scores of busy, large-scale tourist resorts.

The more dramatic Barlavento Coast extends west from Portimão, and is characterized by a twisting shoreline indented with coves and wind-sculpted cliffs. The coast comes to an end at Cabo São Vicente, known to the medieval Portuguese as the End of the World. The west coast of the Algarve is wilder, colder, windier, and considerably emptier, even though it has its fair share of wonderful beaches. Inland you'll find Roman and Moorish monuments, numerous fruit orchards, and the scenic wooded hillsides of the *serras* that separate the Algarve from the Alentejo.

Barlavento Coast

The hardscrabble town of **Sagres** and the area around it are remote, rugged, and desert-like, with only a relative smattering of hotels, restaurants, and other facilities aimed at tourists. It is like the Algarve's outpost, which is precisely why it has so many admirers.

Prince Henry the Navigator established his Navigation School here (though some protest that it was farther east, near Lagos). The town has a picturesque working harbor and a cute little square, Praça República, and is ringed by informal (and, in summer, hopping) nightspots.

The best beaches near Sagres, **Mareta**, **Martinhal**, **Beliche**, **Tonel**, and **Telheiro**, are sheltered and not over-crowded. Beyond the village of Sagres, a great, rocky peninsula hangs above a brooding ocean. Henry and his sailors are said to have set up camp at the **Fortaleza de Sagres** (fortress) that sits on the promontory, though little of the original structure has survived. Inside is a small 16th-century chapel, Nossa Senhora da Graça, and what looks to be a huge stone sun dial, known as the **Rosa dos Ventos** (rose compass).

A couple of kilometers (one mile) west of Sagres are the more authentic remains of another fortress, **Fortaleza do Beliche.** At the tip of the windswept cliffs of **Cabo de São Vicente,** the lighthouse, built in 1904 on the site of a convent chapel, has a beam visible up to 96 km (60 miles) away.

Lagos, the principal resort of the western Algarve, is the rare beach town that offers something for everyone. By night Lagos is lively, with outdoor restaurant terraces and bars,

The promenade in Lagos, a lively town surrounded by beautiful beaches.

and by day it combines a rich historical past with a busy present. Attractive beaches are on the outskirts of town, so it is not a classic resort in the mold of Praia da Rocha.

The well-restored fortress, **Forte da Ponte da Bandeira**, once guarded the entrance to the harbor in the 17th century. Many of the streets rising towards the top of town are narrow, cobbled, and more accustomed to donkeys than rental cars. Though Lagos town still retains a good part of its original walls—most of them from the 16th century, but part-Roman in places—they

Cabo de São Vicentente, a beacon for ships since 1904.

have been rebuilt and expanded over the centuries.

Lagos was an important trading port under the Moors, but the town enjoyed its heyday after the Reconquest, when it was proclaimed the capital of the Algarve. On Rua General Alberta da Silveira, the tiny chapel **Igreja de Santo António,** an exuberant gilt Baroque work and one of the Algarve's finest churches, was rebuilt soon after the earthquake. The entrance to the church is actually through the curious and eclectic museum next door, **Museu Regional de Lagos.** Rooms display sacred art, archaeological remains, the original charter of Lagos, holy vestments, and a bizarre collection of creatures, like a science

XIII
JESUS É DESCIDO DA CRUZ
E DEPOSTO NO REGAÇO DE SUA MÃE

A roadside shrine in Lagos is testament to the devout religiosity of the region.

experiment gone bad: an eight-legged goat kid preserved in formaldehyde, a one-eyed sheep, a cat with two faces.

The main street of Lagos is the charming, cobbled **Rua 25 de Abril,** packed with restaurants, bars, and antiques and ceramics shops. The beaches near Lagos range from **Meia Praia,** 1.6 km (1 mile) to the east, a long (4 km/2 miles) flat stretch, to pocket-sized coves just west of the city. Weird and wonderful rock formations, and steep cliffs that glow orange at sunset, have made them some of the most photographed in Europe; head for **Praia de Dona Ana** and **Praia do Camilo,** both small, pretty, and crowded (street signs indicate the way to each).

At the southern tip, just before the road turns west to Sagres, are the coast's most spectacular sights. **Ponta da Piedade** (Point of Piety) is the mother of all stack and cliff formations along the Algarve, a stunning terracotta family of bridges, terraces, and grottoes.

Portimão, second only to Faro in size in the Algarve, is the most workmanlike town on the coast. But nestled around it are some of the Algarve's finest beaches, and that has transformed the area into one of the coast's most popular resorts. Praia da Rocha and Praia Três Irmãos in particular are lined with hotels and beach-goers.

Most of Portimão's local color is down by the port, a haven of fishing activity. The top fish-canning spot on the Algarve, Portimão is renowned for its restaurants specializing in *sardinhas grelhadas* (grilled sardines). In the center of town, **Largo 1° de Dezembro** is a 19th-century park with 10 splendid blue-and-white *azulejo* benches, each illustrating a pivotal event in the history of Portugal. Along Rua Machado dos Santos is the handsome **Igreja de Nossa Senhora da Conceição**, sitting atop a small hill and incline of steps. The yellow and white church, originally constructed in the 15th century, has a beautiful Gothic portico with carved capitals, though it looks like a colonial church you might find in Brazil, due to its reconstruction and remodeling in the 18th and 19th centuries.

The Castelo dos Mouros remains in Silves as a relic of the city's tenure as the Moorish capital of the Algarve.

From the center of town, head to the waterfront, especially if it's anywhere near time for lunch or dinner. You can almost follow your nose toward the heady aroma of grilled sardines. It will take you to the **dockside**, lined with simple restaurants, one after the other, all serving an abundance of delicious, smoky sardines (and other fresh-caught fish).

Just 3 km (2 miles) down river from Portimão is **Praia da Rocha,** which became a holiday village for wealthy Portuguese families back at the end of the 19th century. It was "discovered" by the British in the 1930s, when this "beach of rocks," strewn with extravagantly shaped eroded stacks, provided an inspirational refuge for writers and intellectuals. The long, 2-km (1-mile) golden beach remains the main attraction. At the very eastern end of the resort, guarding the River Arade, is the historic **Fortaleza de Santa Catarina de Ribamar** (St. Catherine's Fortress), built in 1621 to defend Silves and Portimão against the Moors.

The opposite end of Praia da Rocha's long stretch is known as **Praia do Vau.** The splendid rock formations and coves continue, but this end of the beach is quieter and less developed than the eastern end.

Just west, **Praia de Três Irmãos** is the slightly upscale beach cousin of Praia da Rocha. The eastern end of the beach is a beautiful cove, hemmed in by cliffs and ochre rocks. Beyond it, the beach stretches to **Alvor**, a classic Algarvian fishermen's village. Narrow cobbled streets plunge downhill to a quay and market where boats bob at anchor on a wide, marshy lagoon. At the top of the hill, on Rua da Igreja, is Igreja Matriz, a charming 16th-century church, with a delicately carved Manueline portico, perhaps the finest on the Algarve.

North of Portimão, and extending across the western half of the province, is the **Serra de Monchique**, a mountain range that protects the coast from the hot plains farther north. The *serra* is a verdant landscape of cork, pine, and chestnut trees, and low-lying areas are covered in blankets of colorful wildflowers.

The first stop on the scenic journey along route 266 is the spa village of **Caldas de Monchique,** known since Roman times for its therapeutic waters. North of Caldas, the road weaves uphill quickly, rising 300 m (1,000 ft) in 5 km (3 miles) past terraced farmlands and forests of eucalyptus, oak, and cork. **Monchique** is a small market town, known for its handicrafts and the famous Manueline portico of its 16th-century **Igreja Matriz**.

The road continues upwards, towards **Fóia,** almost 915 m (3,000 ft) above sea level, affording one of the best views in southern Portugal. On a clear day you can see from the bay of Portimão to the Sagres peninsula, and pick out the rocky outcrops of the Lagos beaches.

Silves is the former Moorish capital of the Algarve. More than eight centuries ago, Silves (then known as Chelb) was one of the strongest outposts in 12th-century Arab Iberia, a magnificent city with palaces, gardens, bazaars, and a huge red castle on a hill.

Silves is now just a dusty backwater, but the glorious setting remains. The **Castelo dos Mouros** (Moors' Castle) took shape after the Reconquest, though it preserves distinctly Moorish lines. Next to the castle is the impressive Gothic **Sé Velha** (Old Cathedral) of Silves, built by the liberating Christian crusaders. Opposite the Sé is the 16th-century **Igreja da Misericórdia,** with a classic Manueline-style side door. The imposing **Torreão da Porta da Cidade** (Turret of the City Gate) gives you a good idea of how

seriously defense of the city was taken.

The charming resort of **Carvoeiro,** an archetypal small Barlavento resort**,** has a tiny beach at the bottom of a pretty valley. The original village of Carvoeiro is now fairly commercialized, but to many people it remains one of the coast's most attractive resorts.

Inland, just off the main road, is the attractive little village of **Porches**, with some classic, white Algarvian houses and filigreed chimneys. Porches is famous throughout Portugal for its **hand-painted pottery**, though you won't find much in the village itself. The shops of greatest renown are along the EN 125 route.

Armação de Pêra, one of the longest beaches in the Algarve, has so far survived

One of the most photographed beaches along this stretch is **Nossa Senhora da Rocha** (Our Lady of the Rock). The rock in question is a promontory, boldly jutting out into the sea, surmounted by a little white fishermen's church.

The beach of **Armação de Pêra** is one of the longest in the Algarve—a flat, golden stretch to the east, picturesque rock stacks and small coves to the west. The massive development on the east end of town, though, has pretty much run

The beautiful beach of Coelha, west of Albufeira, is still relatively uncrowded, despite the nearby fishing town's explosive emergence as the leading resort in the Algarve.

roughshod over the natural beauty of the area, all but eclipsing the former fishing village.

Albufeira, at one time a picturesque fishermen's town, has grown wildly in recent years to become the leading resort in the Algarve. Its cliff-top position and labyrinthine street plan provided an easily defensible spot for the Moors, and Albufeira proved one of the last towns to fall during the Reconquest.

Modern Albufeira has fallen prey to mass tourism—bars, cafés, and nightspots pump out music day and night. The excellent beaches west of town are relatively uncrowded. The best are **São Rafael,** and **Coelha**, **Castelo**, and **Galé,** three small, beautiful coves.

One of the most picturesque towns in the province is the lovely village **Alte**, about 30 km (18 miles) north of

Albufeira. The architectural highlight of the village is the beautiful 16th-century Igreja Matriz, entered through a classic Manueline portal. The rest of Alte is the Algarve of picture postcards—white-washed houses along narrow streets, colorful windows, filigreed chimney pots, and red-tiled roofs.

Loosely grouped with Albufeira are beaches to the east. Here, the coastline features the last of the dramatic rock formations that have made the Algarve so famous. **Falésia** is a beautiful beach framed by high cliffs, but to get to it you need to negotiate the grounds of the Sheraton Algarve, whose elevator down to the beach is for guests only. There are more excellent beaches at **Santa Eulalia, Balaia, Praia da Oura,** and **São João.** The center of activity along this beach hinterland is the infamous "strip"—a long street of bustling bars, restaurants, and nightspots leading up to the hilltop area known as Montechoro.

Nearby **Vilamoura** is a wholly planned and sanitized tourist undertaking with high-rise hotels and sprawling villas that line manicured golf courses to the 19th-hole club bar and the Algarve's biggest marina. It's a major draw for

Fishermen still make their living on the Algarve, though the tourist industry rules the region.

those who have their clubs ready for a golfing vacation; several of the Algarve's best courses have been sculpted out of the area.

A little farther west, **Quarteira,** once a quiet fishing village, is today virtually unrecognizable, subsumed under an onslaught of rows and rows of apartment buildings. East of Vilamoura and Quarteira, the terrain begins to change. The rugged, rocky lines of the Barlavento coast west of Faro give way to long flat beaches of the east.

The small crossroads town of **Almancil** has shops, cafés, and businesses, many of which are dedicated to serving English expatriates. A few miles south on the coast are two of the Algarve's most luxurious and exclusive resorts, Vale do Lobo and Quinta do Lago.

> **Is this the right direction to ...?**
> *Vou bem para ...?*

Vale do Lobo is a maze-like villa community with a nice beach and a variety of golf and tennis resort hotels. **Quinta do Lago,** a few miles down the coast, has one of the finest golf courses on the Algarve, designed delicately along the **Ria Formosa Nature Preserve.** The beach can be reached across a long, nostalgic wooden bridge that crosses over wetlands and bird sanctuaries.

Back toward Almancil is one of the Algarve's top attractions. About 16 km (10 miles) west of Faro, a simple white church stands out on a small hill overlooking the thundering highway. A sign simply says "S. Lourenço"—indicating the turn-off to **São Lourenço do Matto** (Church of St. Lawrence of the Woods). Inside is one of the most extraordinary displays of *azulejo* design you'll ever see. Every square inch of the Baroque, 15th-century church—its walls, vaulted ceiling, and cupola—is covered with hand-painted, blue-and-white ceramic tiles. Most date from the

The marina at Vilamoura, a well-planned tourist haven that's especially suited for golf vacations.

early 18th century and depict biblical scenes detailing the life of St. Lawrence. The ensemble is a stunning sight, not to be missed.

Loulé, north of Almancil, is a prosperous town known for its leather, lace, and copper goods. Tour groups come from far and wide to shop at the colorful, bustling market. Just below the permanent market halls on the main Praça da República, you'll find a well-preserved section of the medieval castle walls (which were much damaged by the 1755 earthquake). Also worth visiting are the **Igreja Matriz** (São Clemente), a 13th-century Gothic church with 18th-century *azulejo* tiles; the **Convento da Graça**, with a terrific Manueline portal; and **Ermida de Nossa Senhora da Conceição**, a small church prized for its Baroque altar and ceramic tiles.

In the streets directly below the castle walls, you may well hear the sounds of craftsmen beating copper—from whom you can buy direct. If you are in the Algarve in springtime, don't miss the Loulé Carnival. The parades, "Battle of

Flowers," and musical celebrations are the best of their kind in the region.

São Brás de Alportel is another market town and site of one of only two government *pousadas* (inns) along the Algarve, in the midst of rolling orchards of fig, olive, and orange trees. You may wish to pay a visit to the charming **Museu Etnográfico do Trajo Algárvio** (Museum of Algarvian Costumes), where exhibits of local dress are well staged in a large, old house 90 m (100 yds) or so off the main square.

On the road toward Faro is a pair of historical sights. The **Palácio de Estói** is a most curious find. The charming Rococo palace, found through a small side gate just to the left of the church steps in the town center, once belonged to the Dukes of Estói. Begun in the mid-18th century, it's now abandoned and visibly dilapidated, and only the gardens are open to the public. Yet it is a spectacular sight. Its faded glory includes balustrade terraces and staircases with splendid bursts of bougainvillea, busts of historic characters impaled on the parapets, brightly colored wall tiles, and formal gardens. The Portuguese government aims to construct a *pousada* (inn) here.

> **Azulejos (ah-zoo-lay-zhoos)** are hand-painted, glazed ceramic tiles introduced by the Moors. The name is probably derived from al-zuleiq, Arabic for small polished stone.

The dusty **Villa Romana de Milreu** (Roman ruins of Milreu) are 1.5 km (1 mile) down the road from the village toward Faro (a small sign on the side of the road reads "Ruinas de Milreu"). The tall, semi-circular tower ruin is thought to have been a temple to pagan water gods at one time; however, by the fifth century it had clearly been converted to a church.

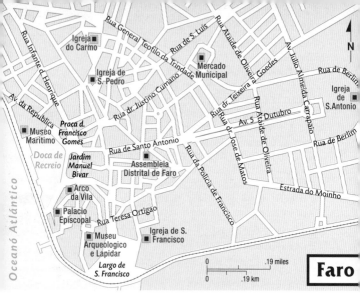

Faro

Faro, the provincial capital of the Algarve, is bypassed by many tourists, though the town has a greater wealth of cultural and historic monuments than any other Algarvian town and a picturesque old quarter.

The main entrance to the circular old town, near the harbor, is the 19th-century **Arco da Vila**, a charming arch and bell tower. Beyond the arch, a cobbled street, worn slick by centuries of tramping feet, leads up to the splendid expanse of the **Largo da Sé** (Cathedral Square)—best seen in the evening when floodlit and free of cars.

The **Sé**'s unusual cathedral tower, main portico, and two interior chapels are all that remain of the original 13th-century Gothic building. Inside is one of the Algarve's most important collections of 17th- and 18th-century

*Only the gardens are open to the public at Palácio de Estói,
where the government has plans to build a pousada.*

sacred art. Climb the tower for fine views over the whole
of Faro.

The **Convento de Nossa Senhora da Assunção**
(Convent of Our Lady of the Assumption), the first
Renaissance building in the Algarve, contains what is
arguably the most beautiful cloister in southern Portugal.
The convent has been beautifully restored as a museum
devoted to archaeology, the **Museu Arqueológico Infante
Dom Henrique.** The principal exhibit is a 2,000-year-old
Roman floor mosaic measuring 9 m (30 ft) long and 3 m
(10 ft) wide.

Central Faro's main thoroughfare is Rua de Santo
António. At its far end is the **Museu Etnográfico**
(Ethnographic Museum), with displays of local handicrafts
and reconstructions of rooms in a typical Algarvian house.

The museum sits on the edge of Faro's Mouraria, or old Moorish quarter. The new town, an expansion dating from the 19th century, is west of here. **Igreja de São Pedro** (Church of St. Peter), built in the 16th century, has a carved Baroque retable and a couple of Rococo chapels.

But Faro's finest church is **Igreja do Carmo** (Carmelite Church). The promise of its twin belltowers and stately façade is matched by a beautiful gilded interior, but the greatest attraction is the macabre **Capela dos Ossos** (Chapel of Bones). This 19th-century curiosity, like a similar chapel in the town of Évora farther north, is constructed of the skulls and bones of monks, unearthed from the friars' cemetery. Depending on your tolerance for such things, it is either fascinating or sick beyond belief.

Mosaics at the Roman ruins of Milrea, first built as a pagan temple, and later converted to a church.

THE SOTAVENTO COAST

Heading east from the provincial capital of Faro, the first settlement of any size you will come to is the colorful fishing town of **Olhão.** Olhão used to be described as the "little white Cubist town of the Algarve," its architecture likened to that of North African towns. The parish church (which also goes by the name of **Nossa Senhora do Rosário**) was founded by King Dom Pedro II in 1698. The small chapel at the rear, **Nossa Senhora dos Aflitos** (Our Lady of the Afflicted), is where women often pray when their fishermen husbands are away at sea.

> **Speed Limits in Portugal**
> Highways: 120 km/h (75 mph)
> Main roads, rural areas:
> 90 km/h (55 mph)
> Urban areas: 50 km/h
> (30 mph)

Instead of the red-tiled roofs and filigreed chimneys seen elsewhere in the Algarve, the Olhão skyline comprises flat-topped roofs of terraces called *açoeitas*. The **Olhão fish market** is one of the Algarve's best, especially famous for its mussels and other shellfish.

With its triumverate of Moorish, Reconquista, and Renaissance roots clearly visible, **Tavira,** one of the true gems of the Algarve, is one of the region's most historically rich cities. In the 1500s, Tavira had the largest population on the Algarve. This tuna-fishing port with its self-assured town of historic churches, imposing classical-style mansions, and beautiful riverfront gardens probably dates back ar least as far as the Phoenicians or the Carthaginians. In fact, its seven-arched stone bridge of Roman origin is still in use.

Tavira's **castle**, in the center of the *casco histórico* (old quarter), was a defensive structure built by the Moors. The walls look directly onto the **Igreja de Santa Maria do**

Castelo (Church of St. Mary of the Castle), most likely built on the site of the old mosque. The Gothic portal is the only original 13th-century element of the building to have survived the devastating 1755 earthquake. Across the square, the ochre-colored former convent, **Convento da Graça**, is being converted into a *pousada* (inn) by the Portuguese government.

Just down the hill, off Rua Galeria near the river, is the beautiful 16th-century **Igreja da Misericórdia** (Church of Mercy), a spectacular Renaissance edifice with a carved portico. **Rua da Liberdade,** Tavira's main street, is lined with stately 16th-century mansions.

A nice excursion from Tavira is to the nearby island **Ilha de Tavira,** where there is a huge and thoroughly appealing

beach backed by sand dunes. Jetties leave from a point, Quatro Águas, a couple of kilometers (one mile) east of town.

Back on the mainland, a turn-off of the main road east (EN-125, still!) of Tavira leads a small number of visitors to **Cacela Velha**, a perfectly enchanting little white-washed village overlooking the sea. It has an 18th-century church,

A fisherman mends his nets in the historically rich town of Tavira.

a telephone booth, a cemetery, an old well, and a handful of well-tended, blue-and-white houses festooned with flowers.

East of here lie the high-rise canyons of **Monte Gordo.** The raison d'être of all the development is a long but not especially attractive sandy beach, which stretches undisturbed for some 10 km (6 miles).

The Guadiana River, which runs into the Atlantic 3 km (2 miles) east of Monte Gordo, served as a natural frontier for some 2,000 years, forming the boundary between the Roman provinces of

Tiled houses lend an added touch of charm to Tavira, a true gem of the Algarve.

Lusitania (Portugal) and Baetica (southern Spain). This geographical context explains the strategic importance of **Castro Marim,** a fortress town occupied by the Moors for five centuries.

A little to the south, the sleepy but quietly dignified town of **Vila Real de Santo António** (the Royal Town of St. Anthony) is the last of the Algarve's beach towns before Spain. The town was built from scratch in just five months in 1774, aping the grid layout of Lisbon's Baixa (lower city). The town square, **Praça do Marquês do Pombal,** is the tour de force of Vila Real, with black-and-white pavement radiating from an obelisk in the center of the square like rays from the sun. Vila Real de Santo António's main appeal is the ferry to **Ayamonte** across the water in Spain. The trip takes just 20 minutes—less time than it would take to drive to and over the new bridge—and the white town of Ayamonte is a fine sight as you approach it from the river. Crossing into Spain, you will need to take your passport.

On Portugal's toll highways, be careful not to enter the Via Verde lane at the toll booth marked by a green "V" and a sign that reads "Reservada Aderentes"; those "Fast Pass" lanes are reserved for cars with magnetic prepaid cards attached to their windshields.

North from Sagres, along the west coast, is the one part of the

The castelos of Castro Marim, a strategic fortress town held by the Moors for some five centuries.

Although standards of dress have relaxed over the years in this Catholic country, when visiting churches in Portugal it's still best not to wear very short shorts, backless dresses or skimpy tank tops.

Algarve that may well escape intensive development, simply because, although the beaches are pleasant and the coastline dramatic, the water is colder and the wind stronger. For those interested in surfing or solitude, this coast may be ideal. **Aljezur**'s ruined Moorish castle looks over the town, which makes a good base for neighboring beaches, such as the enormous rocky cove at **Arrifana** and the wider dune beach of **Monte Clerigo**, both of which also have their own small tourist complexes. Further north, **Odeceixe** is a pretty village set in a small river valley, which continues down to a wide cliff-backed beach at the estuary.

Highlights of Portugal

Lisbon's Alfama & Belém. The first neighborhood is a tangle of alleyways, squares, and fado clubs evoking the Moorish heritage of Lisbon's oldest area; the second, the site of the famous Jerónimos monastery and other monuments attesting to Portugal's Age of Discovery (see page 18).

Sintra (*Estremadura*). Famous town of lush green hills, fanciful Pena palace, spectacular villas, and a Moorish castle high on a hilltop. Just a short drive from Lisbon and near the beaches of the Estoril coast (see page 40).

Coimbra (*Beiras*). Hilltop university city (see page 51) perched above the River Mondego and famous for its varied architecture and good museums. Nearby are Portugal's finest Roman ruins, at Conimbriga (see page 40), and the legendary Buçaco Forest (see page 54).

Serra da Estrêla (*Beiras*). Portugal's highest mountain range, with beautiful scenery, medieval villages like picture-perfect Linhares (see page 57), and historic castles. Good hiking and skiing (see page 51).

Óbidos (*Estremadura*). One of Portugal's most enchanting towns, completely enclosed by impressive 14th-century fortifications, with a pousada within the castle and many photogenic small streets (see page 43).

Alcobaça, Batalha & Tomar. Three of Portugal's most spectacular religious edifices, all within easy reach of each other: Alcobaça's 12th-century Santa Maria monastery, the 14th-century Santa Maria da Vitória abbey in Batalha, and the Convento de Cristo, constructed by the Templar Order, in Tomar.

Porto & the Douro Valley. The long River Douro snakes from the dramatic gorge at Miranda do Douro (see page 85) through the terraced vineyards of Portugal's port-wine country (see page 59) all the way to Porto, the country's fascinating second city, and the wine lodges across the river (see page 61).

Guimarães & Braga (*Minho*). Historic cities of the Minho in northern Portugal. Guimarães (see page tk) is the birthplace of Portugal, a medieval beauty, and Braga (see page tk) the old ecclesiastical center with a church-dominated old town. A short drive from both towns is the ancient *citânia*— Celt-Iberian settlement—of Briteiros (see page 73).

Lima Valley (*Minho*). A scenic valley that runs from the wild and beautiful Peneda-Gerês National Park (see page tk) through the gentle landscapes around river towns (Ponte de Lima; see page tk) and on to the historic beach resort of Viana do Castelo (see page 77).

Évora (*Alentejo*). A handsome city full of historic monuments, from the Roman Temple to the 12th-century Cathedral and "Chapel of Bones," with prehistoric megaliths nearby (see page 92).

Lagos (*Algarve*). A lively resort with a pretty old town and celebrated beaches within easy reach. The best are Praia de Dona Ana and Praia do Camilo, pretty and framed by cliffs, and the most photographed collection of stack and cliff formations along the Algarve, Ponta da Piedade (see page 104).

WHAT TO DO

SHOPPING

Though Portugal has grown considerably more modern and cosmopolitan over the last two decades, it continues to excel at traditional crafts. Small shops and outdoor markets across the country feature intricate works of gold and silver, hand-painted ceramics, and classic wool rugs. Other shoppers will be pleased by the sprouting of chic fashion and jewelry boutiques in Lisbon and Porto, as well as wine shops and cellars stocking Portugal's famous fortified wines. Relative to other European countries, many consumer goods remain somewhat cheaper in Portugal.

What to Buy

Brass, bronze, and copper. Candlesticks, pots and pans, old-fashioned scales, bowls, and trays can be found across Portugal. *Cataplanas* make a delightful decorative or functional souvenir. The Moorish tradition of producing cooking utensils from beaten metal is maintained in the town of Loulé, in the Algarve.

Carpets and Rugs. Attractive and excellently crafted hand-made rugs, mostly from the Alentejo region, have been produced for centuries. Arraiolos wool rugs are colorful and rustic-looking; the small town of the same name has a few dozen small dealers.

Ceramics, Pottery, and Azulejos. Portugal is renowned for its colorful and hand-painted glazed pottery and tiles. You can buy a single blue-and-white tile, an address plaque for your house, or an entire set of plates. Some shops will paint tiles to order or copy a photograph. But remember that ceramics can be heavy and fragile to carry home; inquire about shipping options. Each region has its own distinctive style, ranging from the intricately painted faience animals of Coimbra to the ubiquitous roosters of Barcelos and the black pottery of Chaves. Good places to buy include the Azulejo Museum in Lisbon (see page 31) and the shops along route EN-125 along the Algarve coast, which sell more ceramics and pottery than anywhere else in Portugal. The small town of Porches has two standout shops: Olaria Algarve (Porches Pottery), which has revived and updated long-forgotten Moorish styles, and Casa Algarve. Coimbra's old city is a good place to find ceramics featuring revived 17th–18th-century styles typical of the area.

Cork. Portugal is the world's leading producer of cork. You'll find place mats, intricate sculptures, and other

designs, and it's as light as a feather to take home.

Embroidery. A great many embroidered, items, including tablecloths and napkins, are all over Portugal — especially at street markets. Look for the delicate hand needlework that comes from the island of Madeira — items that are exceedingly well crafted but still comparatively inexpensive.

Jewelry. Filigree work, a legacy of the Moors, is of

A pottery shop in Évora displays its colorful wares both outside and in.

Leather and wooden goods are a common sight at market stalls such as this one in Barcelos.

extremely high quality. Look for silver filigree earrings and brooches, often in the form of flowers or butterflies.

Leather. You can find a very good selection of fashionable, relatively inexpensive shoes and handbags. Leather belts, bags, and shoes are very popular buys. Shoes are just about as fashionable as in Spain and Italy, and are cheaper.

Tax Free

For non-EU residents, the IVA tax (Value Added Tax) imposed on most goods can be refunded on major purchases. Look for the blue-and-white TAX FREE sign in stores. To obtain the rebate, simply fill out a form provided by the shop where you purchase the goods. One copy is kept by the shop; the others must be presented at customs upon departure. The refund can be credited to your credit card at the airport or mailed to your home address after your return.

> **Quánto custa? –**
> **How much is it?**
> **Tem maior/mais**
> **pequeno? – Do you have**
> **a larger/smaller one?**

Music. To enjoy the sounds of Portugal back home, take home a classic fado recording, perhaps by Amália Rodrigues or Carlos Paredes, or a disc of ethereal Portuguese pop by the Lisbon group Madredeus.

Wine. Portugal's wine industry produces not only excellent table wines from regions like Dão, Douro, and Alentejo, but legendary port wine, which comes from the north. The best places to buy are the cellars maintained by all the major producers in Vila Nova de Gaia just across the river from Porto. Given wine's weight and bulk, it's often best to wait until the duty-free shop at the airport.

When & Where to Shop

Most shops are open at least Monday–Friday 9am–1pm and 3–7pm and Saturday 9am–1pm. Modern shopping malls are usually open 10am–midnight or later, and often on Sunday as well. Increasingly, shops also stay open during lunchtime. Country markets start business around 8am and run through mid-afternoon.

A sardine seller — one of a legion at the great agricultural market in Barcelos.

Street markets (*feiras* or *mercados*) are fun for their atmosphere, and the goods for sale include all kinds of crafts, clothing, and food items. In Lisbon, behind São Vicente de Fora church, the *Feira da Ladra* ("Thieves' Market") is held on Tuesday and Saturday. Barcelos holds the country's largest weekly market. The National Craft Fair in Vila do Conde, near Porto (July and August), and the Craft Fair in Lagoa, in the Algarve (August), both display crafts from all over the country.

Major credit cards are accepted in almost all shops in the cities, but less so in the smaller towns. Prices are generally fixed, except in markets.

ENTERTAINMENT

Nighttime entertainment options differ greatly depending on where you are. Lisbon and Porto offer all kinds of live

music, theater, bars, and clubs, and resorts along the Algarve are well-stocked with bars and discos. Smaller towns tend to be much quieter.

Fado. The classic night out in Lisbon still belongs to the *fado* clubs (*casas de fado*) in Alfama or Bairro Alto. Many offer dinner as well as drinks. Fado's origins are unclear; it may

Low-key bars like this one in Aljezur provide a quiet alternative to night clubs.

have developed as a form of mourning for men lost at sea or it may be a relic of the days of slavery — a kind of Iberian blues. Typically a *fado* troupe consists of a woman dressed appropriately in black accompanied by a couple of men playing acoustic guitars. The music is a swell of longing, regret, and nostalgia. You may also hear a man perform the same sort of ballad with a strong, husky voice. The *fado* is much too solemn to be danced, so regional fishermen's and shepherds' dances are sometimes performed to perk things up.

Lisbon clubs to consider include: **Adega Machado** (Rua do Norte, 91); **A Parreirinha da Alfama** (Beco do Espírito Santa, 1); **A Severa** (Rua das Gáveas, 51); and **Senyor Vinho** (Rua do Meio à Lapa).

Along the Algarve, you'll also find "*fado* nights" at bars and hotels. The quality of performances is unlikely to rival the clubs in Lisbon, but you can still get a taste for this quintessentially Portuguese musical expression.

Other Live Music and Performing Arts. Lisbon is home to the greatest number of opera, ballet, and classical concerts (including the Gulbenkian Symphony). Lisbon's cultural scene offers occasional opera, symphony concerts, ballet, and recitals, usually held in winter. The city's opera company is highly regarded by the rest of the world, and the Gulbenkian Foundation (see page 33) maintains its own symphony orchestra and ballet company. Porto (selected as European City of Culture for 2001) is certainly on the upswing, featuring a wide spate of concerts and theater that will likely improve the city's offerings on a permanent basis.

Nightclubs. Lisbon and Porto are both packed with dance clubs and bars that go late into the night, and popular Algarve resorts such as Albufeira and Praia da Rocha throb to a disco beat. Most other towns in Portugal, while offering a reduced roster of low-key bars, tend to be rather quiet at night.

Gambling. Near Lisbon, the Estoril Casino is one of the biggest draws for gamblers. Casinos are also found in the Algarve at Monte Gordo, Vilamoura, and Praia da Rocha, as well as at Figuera da Foz, Espinho, and Póvoa de Varzim. Popular games are baccarat, craps, roulette, blackjack, and slot machines. To be admitted, you must be over 21 and carry a passport.

SPORTS

From swimming and hiking to the challenge of deep-sea fishing, sports enthusiasts have plenty of options in Portugal. The temperate climate in the south also means year-round golf and tennis.

Water Sports

Diving and Snorkeling. There are some three dozen centers along Portugal's long southern coastline that cater to divers. It is especially popular in the western Algarve at Luz, Lagos, and Sagres. Along the Estoril Coast and just off Sesimbra, south of Lisbon, the extraordinarily clear, calm waters are good for snorkeling and scuba diving.

Fishing. All along the coast you will see anglers in boots casting off from the beaches, and others perched on rocks or man-made promontories. A permit is needed for river and lake fishing; details are available from branches of the Portuguese National Tourist Office (see page 169) or the Instituto Florestal (Avenida João Crisóstomo 26, 1000 Lisbon). Angling conditions are generally best in the winter from October to mid-January.

Boats can be rented in Portimão, Faro, Sesimbra, or Setúbal along the Algarve. One of the best deep-sea fish-

Fishermen setting off from the beaches, or perched on promontories, are a common sight along the Algarve coast.

ing spots is around Sesimbra, known for its swordfish. The waters of the Algarve provide some of the best big-game fishing in Europe.

Sailing and boating. Most beaches protected from the open ocean have rowboats, canoes, or pedalos for rent by the hour. Experienced sailors in search of a more seaworthy craft should ask at the local yacht harbor. In the Algarve, dinghies and sailing instruction are available at Praia de Luz, Quinta do Lago, and Portimão. For bigger craft try the marina at Vilamoura or the Carvoeiro Club. Boat cruises are available in virtually every settlement along the Algarve.

Swimming. With great beaches all round the Portuguese coast, opportunities for swimming could not be better. The Algarve has warmer water and more sheltered beaches than the west coast. Lifeguards are not common. Most hotels have swimming pools. Because of pollution along the Estoril Coast, you should not swim any closer to Lisbon than at Estoril itself, which has been granted an EU blue flag (for safe conditions).

No matter your level of ambition or adventure, you'll be able to sail away in Portugal.

Land Sports

Golf. Portugal has emerged as one of the world's top destinations for golfing vacations, with many companies offering all-inclusive vacations. There are top courses around Lisbon (especially Estoril) and a few near Porto, but it is the Algarve which has the lion's share (including some of the finest courses in Europe). Particularly notable are those at Vilamoura and Quinta do Lago. Request the *Sportugal Golfing* brochure from a Portuguese National Tourist Office (see page 169) or pick up a copy of *Algarve Golf Guide,* with information on all of the courses and pro playing tips. Avid golfers should also consider the option of accommodations at a "Golf Hotel." Typically these are

You'll have no trouble finding the greens in Portugal, where a plethora of courses make it the ideal golf destination.

establishments very close to the top golf courses that offer free (or heavily discounted) golf on courses that may otherwise be difficult to get a game on. They also arrange golf tournaments among their guests.

Green fees range from €45–100 for 18 holes. All courses are open to visitors; many require an official handicap certificate, and all require proper dress.

Horseback riding. There are stables all around the country where horses can be hired, and many *quintas* (hotels on country estates) provide horses for guests. The Algarve in particular has a number of riding centers, or *centros hípicos*. Most of the horses you'll encounter are at least part Lusitano, a famous and sure-footed Portuguese breed.

Tennis. Major hotels tend to have their own tennis courts, but there are tennis clubs and public courts as well. Many golf clubs also have their own courts. The Algarve is home to several world-class tennis centers — one of the most impressive is at Vale do Lobo. Another famous center is run by David Lloyd at Clube de Ténis Rocha Brava near Carvoeiro. The Estoril Tennis Club is another excellent center.

Walking. The many national parks in central and northern Portugal are ideal for walking and hiking: The Serra da Estrela and Peneda-Gerês and Montesinho National Parks are three of the best. The beaches and cliffs along the Algarve coast are also excellent for walking, as are the mountains of the Serra do Monchique in Trás-Os-Montes.

Spectator Sports

Bullfights. Portuguese bullfights differ from the Spanish version in one crucial respect: The bull is not killed in the ring, but later in a slaughterhouse.

Portugal's home of bullfighting is Vila Franca de Xira (see page 49) in the Ribatejo. Fights are also staged in the Campo Pequeno Praça de Touros bullring in Lisbon (beginning in May until the end of September, with bullfights presented every Thursday and Sunday) and the Monumental arena in Cascais. Bullfights strictly organized for tourists are held at Lagos, Quarteira, and Vila Real de Santo António, and Albufeira along the Algarve coast during the bullfighting season (look for notices advertising "Praça de Toiros").

The season runs from Easter Sunday to October.

Soccer (football). As in most European countries, *futébol* draws big crowds in Portugal. Lisbon's two major teams are Benfica and Sporting Clube de Portugal. FC Porto is the top

club in Portugal's second city. The Algarve has a team in
Farense, from the regional capital. Check with local tourism
offices for a schedule of matches.

PORTUGAL FOR CHILDREN

The most popular destination for children is likely to be the
beach. Most hotels also have pools, many with shallower
pools for children.

The beaches of the Algarve, with long, sandy, gently
shelving beaches for small children and small rocky coves
ideal for older children to explore, are perfect for family holidays. Pay attention to the beach warning flags, however.
Green means the sea is calm and a lifeguard is on duty;
green plus a checkered flag means that no lifeguard is on
duty; yellow urges caution; red means danger and warns
bathers to stay ashore.

The biggest new attraction in Lisbon for children is the
Parque das Nações (see page 37), with its splendid aquarium (Oceanário de Lisboa), playgrounds, fountains, paddle-
boats, and aerial cable cars.

Portugal dos Pequinitos, in Coimbra (see page 53), is a
theme park of miniatures of Portugal's most famous buildings. The narrow-gauge railways of the north also make a
fun day-trip.

The Algarve also has the most standard facilities for
children, such as theme parks, zoos and waterparks. The
best waterparks are reputed to be **Slide & Splash** (EN-125
Vale de Deus, near Lagoa) and **The Big One** (En-125, near
Alcantarilha). Another attraction is **Zoomarine** (EN-125,
km 25), a small amusement park with performing dolphins
and sea lions, a parrot show, a mini-zoo, a cinema, various
children's fairground rides, and swimming pools.

Calendar of Festivals and Events

Portugal has innumerable festivals, fairs, and markets, though the folk festivals are modest compared with such international spectacles as the Carnival in Rio or the running of bulls in Pamplona. The most colorful religious processions are in northern Portugal, especially in Braga.

A fuller list of events and information on precise dates can be obtained from the Portuguese Tourist Board or its web site <www.portugal.org> (see page 169).

February–March

Carnival (Mardi Gras), with processions and fireworks all round the country. Most popular in Ovar, Nazaré, Torres Vedras, Funchal, and Loulé.

Lisbon: Fado Festival at various sites.

March–April

Holy Week processions, including famed Pilgrimage to Bom Jesus in Braga.

May

Barcelos: Feast of the Crosses music concerts and a spectacular display of fireworks on the Cávado River; first weekend.

Fátima: First pilgrimage of year to shrine 13 May.

Coimbra: "Queima das Fitas" (ceremonial burning of ribbons) celebration marking the end of the university's academic year.

Algarve: International Music Festival throughout month at various sites.

June–July

Lisbon: Festival of music, dance, and theater all month. Fairs and festivities for the People's Saints, honoring St. Anthony (13 June), St. John (24 June), and St. Peter (29 June).

Vila do Conde: Festa do Corpo de Deus procession in the historic section of town with the streets covered in flowers.

Vila Franca de Xira (north of Lisbon): Running of bulls through the streets the first two Sundays of July.

July–August
Estoril/Cascais: Estoril International Music Festival.

August
Guimarães: "Festas Gualterianas" (3-day festival dating to 15th century, with torch-lit religious processions, bands, folk dance groups, and colorful medieval parade) (4–6 Aug.)

Viana do Castelo: Festa da Nossa Senhora da Agonia (Our Lady of Agony Festivities): famous religious festival with traditional costumes and fireworks over the river. (weekend nearest to the 20th).

September
Lamego: Festivities honoring Nossa Senhora dos Remédios (annual pilgrimage to famous Baroque shrine, along with torchlight procession, folklore festival, fairs, and fireworks, culminating with triumphal procession). (6–9 Sept)

Nazaré: Our Lady of Nazaré (Nossa Senhora da Nazaré): fishermen carry an image of the town's patron saint on their shoulders in festive processions; also bullfights, fairs, concerts, folk dancing, and singing. (2nd week Sept).

October
Fátima: Last Pilgrimage of year to shrine (pilgrims celebrate the last apparition of the Virgin to shepherds on 12 October 1917) (12–13 October)

Vila Franca de Xira: October Fair: ancient fair that includes bull running, fair, and bullfights (first two weeks).

November
Golegã: National Horse Show/Saint Martin's Fair (2nd week).

December
Lisbon: Bolsa de Natal Christmas market (throughout city).

EATING OUT

Portuguese cuisine is true to its origins, the food of fishermen and farmers. Traditional dishes are found in both expensive restaurants and the simplest of cafés. But the Portuguese can also be very inventive; you're likely to sample combinations like clams and pork, sole and bananas, or pork and figs.

Seafood fans are in luck in Portugal, with a surfeit of just-caught fish and shellfish. The humble but noble Portuguese sardine is an inexpensive standard, especially down south, and with a hunk of local rustic bread and a bottle of house wine, you can still feast well on a small budget. Not that restaurants skimp on meat: you can find delicious pork and lamb dishes and steak. You'll also enjoy freshly picked fruit and vegetables, not to mention Portuguese wines, which are eminently drinkable.

> When trying to decide which bathroom door to enter, look for the words Senhoras (ladies) and Homens (men).

Some of the best dishes are regional stews, such as the ensopadas of the Alentejo, the caldeiradas of the Algarve, and the açordas of Estremadura. These dishes are found in restaurants all over the country.

Portions in Portuguese restaurants tend to be rather large. You can also ask for a half portion (uma meia dose) which is usually charged at around two-thirds the full price.

Restaurants and Menus

Menus displayed in the window or beside the door let you know what to expect in variety and price. Prices normally include taxes and a service charge, but it's customary to leave an additional tip of between 5% and 10% for good service. *Típico* restaurants specialize in local cuisine, marisqueiras feature seafood, and churrasqueiras offer barbecue.

The Tourist Menu

Many restaurants and cafés offer an *ementa turística* — literally, "tourist menu." However, the term doesn't connote a poor-grade international tourist meal. Rather, it is an economically priced set meal — typically bread, butter, soup, main course, and dessert. Another inexpensive option at many restaurants and cafés is the *prato do dia* (dish of the day).

Eat while you sightsee — riverside restaurant are a relaxing diversion at Tavira.

Meal times

Breakfast (pequeno almoço) is usually eaten any time up until about 10am. Lunch (almoço) is served from shortly after noon until 3pm, and dinner (jantar) runs from 7:30–10pm (or later in a casa de fado). Snacks between meals are usually eaten at a pastelaria (pastry and cake shop), salão de chá (tea shop), or what the Portuguese call by its English name, a snack bar [md] a stand-up counter selling sandwiches, savory pastries, and sweets.

Local Specialties

Soups and Starters. Lunch and dinner often get off to a hearty start, and soups are typical Portuguese fare. Caldo verde (green soup) is a thick broth of potato purée with finely-shredded cabbage or kale. Fans of smoked food have two treats to look for. The first is smoked ham (*presunto fumado*) — the best comes from Chaves, the northernmost province of Portugal (although Monchique ham is also highly regarded). The second is smoked swordfish (*espadarte fumado*), a little like smoked salmon but with a grainier texture and less sweet.

Seafood

The best advertisement for seafood is usually the window of a restaurant: a generous refrigerated display case with crabs and prawns, oysters and mussels, sea bass and sole. Seafood restaurants generally sell shellfish by weight, giving the price in euros per kilo. You may wish to have a calculator handy, or be sure they give you the price in easier-to-calculate Euros. The Portuguese are very fond of boiled fish dishes, usually served with generous portions of cabbage and boiled potatoes and doused with a little oil and vinegar.

A number of seafood dishes are true local specialties. *Caldeirada* is a rich seafood stew. *Amêijoas na cataplana* is an invention from the Algarve of steamed mussels (or clams) with sausages, tomato, white wine, ham, onion, and herbs.

Along the cobbled streets of Lagos, take a break for a bite and a breather.

Açorda de marisco is a spicy, garlic-scented thick bread-soup full of seafood bits; raw eggs are later added into the mixture. *Lulas recheadas* are squid stuffed with rice, olives, tomato, onion, and herbs. *Sardinhas* (sardines) are excellent and often served grilled (*sardinhas assadas*).

Bacalhau, cod, is the national dish of Portugal, even though it can be expensive and comes dried and salted and from distant seas, including Canada and Norway. The Portuguese say that cod is served in 100, 365, or 1,000 different ways (depending on the teller's taste for hyperbole). For many people, bacalhau is an acquired taste. For those unconvinced of its attributes, the best way to try it is in Bacalhau à Gomes de Sá, in which flaky chunks are baked with parsley, potatoes, onion, and olives and garnished with grated hard-boiled egg.

A menu that quotes a price as "preço V." means variable, or market, price. Be sure to clarify the day's market price before ordering.

Fresh fish, whole or filleted, is usually served grilled, as are outstanding *atum* (tuna) and espadarte, swordfish steaks. For those who know some Spanish or Portuguese, *peixe espada* might sound like swordfish; however, it is actually scabbard fish, a long, thin fish that comes from the area south of Lisbon.

Meat

Bife na frigideira is not what you might think. Frigideira means frying pan, and this dish is a beefsteak nicely done in a wine sauce. *Cabrito assado* is baked goat kid served with rice and potato, heavy-going but delicious. *Carne de porco à Alentejana* is an inspired dish of clams and pork cooked with paprika and garlic. *Espetada mista* means Portuguese shish kebab: chunks of beef, lamb, and pork on a

spit. Feijoada is the national dish of Brazil, the former Portuguese colony. In Portugal, it's not nearly as elaborate or ritualized, but it's still a hearty and tasty stew of pigs' feet and sausage, white beans, and cabbage. Most meat dishes in Portugal are served with both rice and potatoes.

Game and Fowl. *Frango* (chicken) is popular and versatile, be it stewed in wine sauce, fried, roasted, or barbecued to a tasty crisp. Some restaurants specialize in game — *codorniz* (quail), *perdiz* (partridge), *lebre* (hare), and even *javali* (wild boar).

There's no shortage of bacalhau at the bustling Barcelos agricultural fair.

International & Exotic Cuisine. Thanks to Portugal's imperial legacy, you can experiment while you're in Lisbon. The former colony of Goa accounts for the local popularity of *caril* (curry) and other Indian-style dishes.

Piri-piri is a hot-pepper condiment and preparation from Angola that will set most mouths ablaze. Order a piri-piri dish with extreme caution.

Vegetarian Dishes. Vegetarianism has made few inroads in Portugal, and there are few vegetarian restaurants outside the capital and the Algarve. However, good fresh vegetables are often

> May I have the bill?
> **Pode me dar a conta?**

142

served as side dishes, including the popular broad beans (favas). Salads are readily available.

Salada à Portuguesa is made with green peppers, garlic, tomato, and cucumber. If you eat eggs, omelettes are served everywhere.

Dessert and Cheese. The Portuguese sweet tooth may be a little too much for your taste. Locals pour sugar on a sliced sweet orange, after all. The cakes, custards, and pastries are usually made with the basics, egg yolks and sugar, and are delicious. *Pudim flã* (also flam, flan, or flão) is the Portuguese version of the Spanish flan (caramel custard).

The richest and most expensive cheese in Portugal is Serra da Estrela, a delicious cured ewes' milk cheese that originates high up in the mountains. Also on many menus is Flamengo, a mild cheese and very similar to Edam.

Some restaurants serve queijo fresco as an appetizer. This is a small, white, soft mini-cheese made of ewe's and goat's milk, and is so bland you'll want to add pepper and salt.

Drinks

Table Wines. Portuguese wines, while not as well known as those from Spain and France, are uniformly

A beautiful cluster of sausage hangs at the Saturday market in Loule.

quite good, and several regions produce truly excellent wines. Several of the best wine-producing regions have names whose use is controlled by law (região demarcada). Look for wines from Dão, Douro, or Alentejo demarcated regions, or simply tell the waiter tinto (red) or branco (white), the practice of many Portuguese diners.

Vinho espumante is Portuguese sparkling wine, packaged in a Champagne-shaped bottle. Most are sweetish but you can also find some quite dry versions.

The two most celebrated Portuguese wines, port and Madeira, are mostly known as dessert wines, but they may also be sipped as aperitifs. The before-dinner varieties are dry or extra dry white port and the dry Madeiras, Sercial and Verdelho. After dinner, sip one of the famous ruby or tawny ports (aged tawnys are especially good) or a Madeira dessert wine, Boal or Malvasia (Malmsey).

Other Drinks. Portuguese beers are good and refreshing. Light or dark, they are served chilled, bottled, or from the tap. One of the best and most common is Sagres. You can find various brands of mineral water in small or large bottles, bubbly or still. Portuguese fruit juices can be delicious, and well-known soft drinks are also available.

menu - **a carta**	
pre-fixe meal - **ementa turística**	
wine list - **carta de vinhos**	
the bill - **a conta**	

Menu Reader

To Help You Order...

We'd like a table?	**Queríamos uma mesa.**		
I'd like a/an/some ...	**Queria ...**		
beer	**cerveja**	fish	**peixe**
mineral water	**água mineral**	rice	**arroz**
(sparkling)	**com gás**	fruit	**fruta**

(still)	**sem gás**	salad	**salada**
bill	**a conta**	ice cream	**gelado**
bread	**pão**	salt	**sal**
butter	**manteiga**	meat	**carne**
napkin	**guardanapo**	sandwich	**sanduíche**
menu	**ementa**	wine	**vinho**
coffee	**um café**	soup	**sopa**
pepper	**pimenta**	milk	**leite**
dessert	**sobre mesa**	sugar	**açúcar**
tea	**chá**	potatoes	**batatas**

...and Read the Menu

alho	garlic	**frito**	fried
amêijoas	baby clams	**grão de bico**	chick-pea
ananás	pineapple	**guisado**	stew
assado	roast	**laranja**	orange
atun	tuna	**legumes**	vegetables
azeitonas	olives	**leitão**	suckling pig
bacalhau	cod (salted)	**linguado**	sole
besugo	sea-bream	**lombo**	fillet
bife (vaca)	steak (beef)	**lulas**	squid
bolo	cake	**maçã**	apple
borrego	lamb	**mariscos**	shellfish
camarões	shrimp	**mexilhões**	mussels
caranguejo	crab	**molho**	sauce
cavala	mackerel	**morangos**	strawberries
cebola	onion	**ostras**	oysters
chouriço	spicy sausage	**evo**	egg
churrasco	grilled meat	**pargo**	bream
coelho	rabbit	**pescada**	hake
cogumelos	mushrooms	**pescadinha**	whiting
costeletas	chops	**pêssego**	peach
couve	cabbage	**porco**	pork
cozido	boiled	**presunto**	ham
dobrada	tripe	**queijo**	cheese

145

HANDY TRAVEL TIPS

An A–Z Summary of Practical Information

Listed after most main entries is an appropriate Portuguese translation, usually in the singular. You'll find this vocabulary useful when asking for information or assistance.

A

ACCOMMODATION (See also CAMPING; YOUTH HOSTELS; and Recommended Hotels on page 172.)

Except for family-run *hotéis rurais* (rural hotels), hotels in Portugal are graded from 2-star to 5-star deluxe. Rates are lower in less elaborate hostelries: an *estalagem* or inn; a *pensão* (rooms with meals available); or *residencial* (rooms, generally without meals). Confusingly, even some elite, intimate inns in Lisbon are often referred to as a pensão.

Pousadas (like Spanish paradors) are state-run inns, usually in historic buildings and scenic sites; their restaurants are usually among the town's best, with special attention given to local food and wine. Ask at the tourist offices (see page 169) for a detailed list, or visit the website, <www.pousadas.pt>.

Portugal's **Turismo de Habitação** (also called "Solares de Portugal") system began in the Minho and has spread over much of the country. People offer rooms in privately-owned *quintas* (country houses and rural estates) and *solares* (manor houses). Breakfast is included; often there are sporting facilities. You can book directly with the host or through Turihab (Praça da República, 4990 Ponte de Lima, Portugal; Tel. 258/74 16 72; fax 258/74 14 44; <www.sidra.pt/turihab>). The Portuguese National Tourist Offices (see page 169) can also provide information on the various options available.

I'd like a single/ double room.	**Queria um quarto simples/duplo.**
with bath/shower	**com banho/chuveiro**
What is the rate per night?	**Qual é o preço por noite?**

Portugal

AIRPORTS (*aeroporto*)

Portugal has three international airports: Lisbon, Faro, and Porto.

The **Aeroporto de Lisboa** is only 4 miles from the city center, a 15-minute drive (allow twice as long at rush hour). Besides taxis, which are plentiful (see PUBLIC TRANSPORTATION on page 165) and charge about €10 to the center of Lisbon, you can take bus 91, the airport shuttle, which leaves about every 20 minutes from 7am–9pm. They pass through the city center, including the Rossio, on the way to Cais do Sodré train station. The ticket can be used all day on trams and buses (though not the Metró subway).

For information on flight times call Tel. 21/840 20 60; the main airport number is Tel. 21/848 11 01 and for airport information, Tel. 21/840 22 62.

Faro International Airport, serving the Algarve, is 7 km (4 miles) from Faro, the regional capital. It's a 10-minute taxi ride to Faro, and about half an hour by car to Albufeira. There's also a bus service to Faro. Several international and local car rental agencies have service desks at the airport. Helpful staff at the airport tourist information office will assist you with finding accommodation and any other queries you may have. Elsewhere in the terminal are a post office, bank, ATM machine, restaurant/bar, newsstand, souvenir shop, and duty-free shop. For airport information, call Tel. 289/808 080 (arrival and departure times: Tel. 289/800 801).

Porto's Francisco Sá Carneiro airport lies about 20 minutes north of the town, towards Matasinhos. The facilities are similar to those at Faro. Aerobus, Bus 56 and taxis to the center. For information, Tel. 222/948 21 41.TAP Air Portugal information is Tel. 0808/205 700.

Where do I get the bus to the airport/ center of the city?	**Onde posso apanhar o autocarro para o aeroporto/ centro da cidade?**

B

BUDGETING FOR YOUR TRIP

With a favorable exchange rate, Portugal may well be cheaper than many other European destinations. However, the season when you go will have much to do with the cost of your trip. Hotel rates rise astonishingly during the summer months.

Transportation to Portugal. For Europeans, Lisbon and Porto are a short, direct flight away, usually 2–3 hours. Regularly scheduled flights may not be inexpensive, but you are likely to find a fair choice of discounts and charter flights, especially from London. For those traveling from beyond Europe, the flight will be a considerably greater expenditure and portion of your overall budget, though you may also be able to find packages and specials. Many Europeans fly direct to Faro aboard regularly scheduled and charter flights. Scheduled flights from England and continental Europe may cost anywhere from $300 to $600 roundtrip. Scheduled flights from North America can often be had for $500–$600 roundtrip outside of high season. Economical package deals—airline and hotel—are usually available, considerably reducing the percentage of the flight in your budget.

Accommodation. Hotels at the top levels are comparable to those in large European cities. There is a huge difference in rack (official) rates according to season. In high summer season (July–August especially) in the Algarve, hotel prices are exorbitant — often double what they cost in off-season. In high season, a double room with bath per night in a 3-star hotel averages €50–75; 4-star hotel, €85–125; 5-star hotel, €150–300. *Pousadas* generally range from €100–150 for a double room.

Keep in mind that most do not include breakfast or the $17^{1}/2\%$ IVA (value added) tax.

Meals. Even top-rated restaurants may be surprisingly affordable compared to most European cities. Portuguese wines are quite good and very attractively priced, even in fine restaurants. A 3-course meal with wine in a reasonable establishment averages about €12.50–25 per person. Portugal, like Spain, offers a midday meal bargain, the *ementa turística*, often costing no more than €10–15 for a prix-fixe 3-course meal.

Local transportation. Buses and taxis are reasonably priced. Local buses are less than €1.50; a taxi costs between €2.50–5 for most fares within a resort or town (a supplement of 20% is levied on weekends, public holidays, and between 10pm and 7am). Taxis can be hired for day trips for set fees; check with the local tourist office for a list of trips.

Portugal

Incidentals. Your major expenses will primarily be excursions, sporting activities, and entertainment, unless these are included in the hotel or package deal that you paid for.

Renting a car to travel is a good idea to allow yourself maximum flexibility, but be sure to budget for the cost of a rental as well as gas. This can be costly, as it is throughout most of Europe. Economy-class car rental is cheaper than in most parts of Europe; expect it to run between €30–40 per day (including collision insurance and the requisite taxes). You may find even better bargains at local firms. Gas (petrol) per liter is unleaded around €1.00, diesel €0.65.

Nightlife and entertainment costs vary widely. Expect cover fees at discos to range from €7.50–15 (usually includes first drink); casino entrance, €10.

C

CAMPING (*campismo*)

There are dozens of sites all over the country. Information on camping can be obtained from tourist offices (see page 169), or the Federação Portuguesa de Campismo, Av. 5 de Outubro no. 15, 3rd Floor; Tel. 21/315 27 15; fax 21/54 93 72. Check the web site <www.portugal-insite.pt> for a detailed list of 20 campsites throughout the Algarve (click on the individual site for features).

You can only camp at recognized sites, and not on beaches or in forests. Some natural parks require camping permits and some sites require membership of an international camping organization. You will also have to produce a passport.

Is there a campsite near here?	**Há algun parque de campismo por aqui perto?**
May we camp here?	**Podemos acampar aqui?**
We have a caravan (trailer).	**Temos uma roulotte.**

CAR RENTAL (*carros de aluguer*) (See also DRIVING)

International and local firms operate in major cities and the major tourist areas. The minimum age for renting a car is generally 21, and you must have a valid license held for at least one year. Most rental companies will accept your home country national driver's license. Third-party insurance is included in the basic charge, but a collision damage waiver and personal accident policy may be added at an additional cost.

If you wish to travel a good deal at your leisure, renting a car is advisable. Major international companies — Avis, Hertz, Budget, National, Europcar — are located in airports and in major cities; sometimes they have small satellite offices in other towns. Rates are usually lower if contracted and paid for in advance in one's home country. Ask for special seasonal rates and discounts and find out what insurance is included.

A value-added tax (IVA) is added to the total charge, but will have been included if you have pre-paid the car rental before arrival (normally the way to obtain the lowest rates). Third-party insurance is required and included, but full collision coverage is advisable as well. Many credit cards automatically include this if you use the card to pay for the car, but be sure to verify this before departure. Renting at an airport may incur a surcharge.

I'd like to rent a car today/ tomorrow.	**Queria alugar um carro para hoje/amanhã.**
for one day/a week	**por um dia/uma semana**
Please include full insurance.	**Que inclua um seguro contra todos os riscos, por favor.**

CLIMATE (*clima*)

Portugal's climate is kind, especially in the exceptionally sunny Algarve. Summers are warm and winters mild. Farther north the weather can be cold in winter, especially in the interior mountains.

The following chart shows the average air and sea temperatures:

Portugal

	Jan	Mar	May	July	Sept	Nov
Lisbon						
Air temp. °C/°F	11/52	14/57	17/63	22/72	22/72	14/57
Sea temp. °C/°F	15/59	17/63	19/66	21/70	19/66	16/61
Faro						
Air temp. °C/°F	12/54	13/55	18/65	24/75	22/72	16/61
Sea temp. °C/°F	15/59	17/63	19/66	21/70	19/66	16/61
Bragança						
Air temp. °C/°F	4/39	8/47	13/55	21/70	17/63	8/46

CLOTHING (*roupa*)

The Algarve has a Mediterranean climate and you may find a sweater will be needed for some evenings. Farther north, warmer clothes may be necessary, especially if you are going inland or to mountainous regions. Most restaurants are informal, but you may want to bring a jacket and tie for grander establishments.

Will I need a tie?	**É preciso gravata?**
Is it all right if I wear this?	**Vou bem assim?**

CRIME AND SAFETY (*delito*) (See also EMERGENCIES and POLICE)

Portugal in general is a safe country. Major tourist areas such as the Algarve experience more petty crime than other parts of Portugal, though crimes involving violence against tourists are very rare. Theft from rental cars is the most common crime targeting tourists. In rural areas the problem is far less acute, but in resorts and where cars are left unattended for a period of time (at beach parking lots, scenic spots, etc.) the risk is high.

Burglaries of vacation apartments, though less common than car theft, also occur, so be on your guard to the extent possible.

As a general rule, never leave anything in your car, even if it is out of sight and locked in the trunk (boot). Keep valuables in the hotel safe and refrain from carrying large sums of money or expensive jewelry on the street. Do not leave purses and cameras unattended on the beach.

Report any theft to the hotel receptionist, the nearest police station, or the local tourist office. You must report any losses to the local police within 24 hours and obtain a copy of your statement for insurance purposes.

Lisbon is infamous for its pickpockets, particularly on the Metrò and Rossio square. You are also advised not to walk in the Bairro Alto or Alfama areas at night unless in a group.

I want to report a theft.   **Quero participar um roubo.**

CUSTOMS AND ENTRY REQUIREMENTS (*alfândega*)
American, British, Canadian, and many other nationalities need only a valid passport — no visa — to visit Portugal. EU nationals may enter with an identity card. The length of stay authorized for most tourists is 90 days (60 for US and Canadian citizens).

The Portuguese-Spanish border scarcely serves as a frontier anymore and visitors can come and go easily, though you should carry your passport.

Currency restrictions. Visitors from abroad can bring in (or exit with) any amount of euros or foreign currency, but sums exceeding the equivalent of €12,500 in foreign currency must be declared upon arrival in Portugal.

Customs. Free exchange of non-duty-free goods for personal use is permitted between Portugal and other EU countries. However, duty-free items still are subject to restrictions: Check before you go.

I've nothing to declare.   **Não tenho nada a declarar.**
It's for my personal use.   **É para uso pessoal.**

D

DRIVING (See also CAR RENTAL and EMERGENCIES)
If you take your own car, you'll need your national driver's license, registration papers, and insurance — third-party coverage is obligatory. The Green Card makes it valid in other countries.

Portugal

Road conditions. The rules of the road are the same as in most western European countries. At roundabouts (traffic circles) the vehicle in the circle has priority unless road markings or lights indicate otherwise. Seat belts are compulsory. Local driving standards are improving but are still erratic. In towns, pedestrians nominally have priority at crosswalks — but if you're walking, don't count on it!

Speed limits are 120kph (75mph) on motorways, 90kph (56mph) on other roads, and 50kph (37mph) in urban areas. Minimum speeds are posted (in blue) for some motorway lanes and suspension bridges. Cars towing caravans (trailers) are restricted to 50kph (31mph) in towns and 70kph (45mph) on the open road and motorways (portagem). Most motorways have tolls. The Portuguese routinely appear to disregard speed limits, but that doesn't mean you should.

Fuel Costs. Fuel by the liter is expensive in Portugal, as it is throughout Western Europe. Prices, controlled by the government, should be the same — or very close to it — everywhere you go. Many gas stations are 24-hour, and all accept credit cards. Use the following charts for help with gas mileage.

Fluid measures

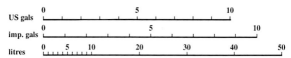

Distance

Parking. You have to park facing the same direction as the flow of traffic on that side of the road. Unless there's an indication to the contrary, you can park for as long as you wish. Certain areas are metered and others are "Blue Zones," where you must buy a ticket from a machine. Parking lots and garages are also available.

If You Need Help. If you belong to an automobile organization affil-
iated with the Automóvel Clube de Portugal (Rua Rosa Araújo 24,
Lisbon; Tel. 21/356 39 31), you can use their emergency and repair
services free of charge. Otherwise, most garages in Portugal can han-
dle the usual problems.

Road signs. Standard international pictograms are used in Portugal,
but you might also encounter the following signs:

Alto	Stop
Cruzamento	Crossroads
Curva perigosa	Dangerous bend (curve)
Descida ingreme	Steep hill
Desvio	Detour (Diversion)
Encruzilhada	Crossroads
Estacionamento permitido	Parking allowed
Estacionamento proíbido	No parking
Guiar com cuidado	Drive with care
Obras/Fim de obras	Road works (men working)/ end of road works
Paragem de autocarro	Bus stop
Pare	Stop
Passagem proíbida	No entry
Pedestres/peões	Pedestrians
Perigo	Danger
Posto de socorros	First-aid post
Proibida a entrada	No entry
Saída de camiões	Truck exit
Seguir pela direita/esquerda	Keep right/left
Sem saída	No through road
Sentido proíbido	No entry
Sentido único	One-way street
Silêncio	Silence zone
Stop	Stop
Trabalhos	Road works (men working)
Trânsito proíbido	No through traffic
Veículos pesados	Heavy vehicles
Velocidade máxima	Maximum speed

Are we on the right road for …?	**É esta a estrada para …?**
Fill the tank, please, super.	**Encha o depósito de super, por favor**.
Check the oil/tires/ battery, please.	**Verifique o óleo/os pneus/ a bateria, se faz favor.**
I've broken down.	**O meu carro está avariado.**
There's been an accident.	**Houve um acidente.**

E

ELECTRICITY (*corrente eléctrica*)

Standard throughout Portugal is 220-volt, 50-cycle AC. For US appliances, 220-volt transformers and plug adaptors are needed.

| I need an adaptor/ a battery, please. | **Preciso de um adaptador/ uma pilha, por favor.** |

EMBASSIES AND CONSULATES (*consulado; embaixada*)

Embassies are listed in local phone books (under *Consulado* or *Embaixada*). Most are in Lisbon, Porto, or Faro.

Embassies in Lisbon:

Australia (use UK Embassy): Rua de São Bernardo 33; Tel. 21/392 40 00.

Canada (Embassy/Consulate): Avenida da Liberdade 144, 3°; Tel. 21/347 48 92.

Republic of Ireland (Embassy/Consulate): Rua da Imprensa à Estrela 1, 4°; Tel. 21/396 15 69.

South Africa (Embassy): Avenida Luís Bivar 10/10 A; Tel. 21/353 50 41.

UK (Embassy): Rua de São Bernardo 33; Tel. 21/392 44 00.

US (Embassy/Consulate): Avenida das Forças Armadas 16; Tel. 21/727 33 00.

A number of European countries have consuls or honorary consuls in the Algarve. For more serious matters, people are usually referred to their embassy in Lisbon.

British consulate (Consulado da Grã Bretanha, which handles Commonwealth nationals, including Australians and New Zealanders): Largo Francisco A Maurício, 7-1; Portimão; Tel. 282/417 800.

Canadian consulate (Consulado de Canadá): Rua Aboim Ascensão, 87; Faro; Tel. 289/880 880).

Most embassies and consulates are open Mon–Fri from 9 or 10am until 5pm, with a break in the middle of the day of 1-2^1/$_2$ hours.

Where's the British/ American embassy?	**Onde é a embaixada inglesa/americana?**
It's very urgent.	**É muito urgente.**

EMERGENCIES (*urgência*) (See also HEALTH AND MEDICAL CARE and DRIVING)

The following free numbers are useful 24-hours a day in an emergency:

General emergency	**112**
Fire	**60 60 60**
Ambulance (Red Cross)	**301 77 77**

Although you can call the police from any one of the blue boxes in the street marked *polícia*, it's unlikely you'll get anyone on the other end who speaks anything but Portuguese.

G

GAY and LESBIAN TRAVELERS

In a country heavily influenced by the Catholic Church, attitudes towards gays are not as tolerant as elsewhere in Europe. Lisbon is the most important city in Portugal's gay scene and offers a number of bars and clubs catering to a gay crowd. In certain enclaves of the Algarve, such as "the Strip" in Albufeira, gay travelers will find accommodating bars and restaurants. A web site, <www.portugal-gay.pt>, contains a travel guide for gays and lesbians, with information in English and other languages.

Portugal

GETTING TO PORTUGAL (See also AIRPORTS)

Air Travel. Lisbon's and Porto's airports are linked by regularly scheduled daily non-stop flights from several European cities. There are also direct flights to Lisbon from the US and Canada. From Australia and New Zealand, the usual pattern is to go through London or another European capital. Regularly scheduled, cheap charter flights to Faro (mostly in summer) are available from the UK, Ireland, and most major cities in Western Europe. Scheduled flights by TAP Air Portugal and British Airways are more expensive, though they usually offer special deals outside of high season. Booking ahead is always helpful.

TAP/Air Portugal (Tel. 888/328 26 71 anywhere in Portugal; Lisbon, Tel. 21/841 69 90; New York, Tel. 212/969-5775; London, Tel. 171/828-0262) is the national Portuguese airline. From the US to Lisbon, it flies direct daily from New York and Newark, and once a week from Boston. Continental flies direct to Lisbon from Newark and TWA flies from New York's JFK airport. These and many other airlines make connections in Lisbon and travel on to Faro. Travelers starting their trip in Canada, Australia, New Zealand, or South Africa will make connections to Lisbon or Faro in London or another major European city.

The Lisbon international airport (Tel. 21/840 22 62) is four miles outside of town. Faro International Airport (Tel. 289/808 080), serving the Algarve, is 7 km (4 miles) from Faro, the regional capital. Porto's Fransisco Sá Carneiro (Tel. 222/948 21 41) airport is north of town.

By Car. Many travelers each year arriving for long stays in Portugal take their cars from other points in Europe by major motorways through Spain and Portugal. British travelers can take their car across the Channel to France or Belgium and make the drive from there, although the trip would likely last three or four days. See the information below on ferries, under "By Sea."

The main access road to Lisbon and the Algarve from France, through Spain, is at the western end of the Pyrenees. A motorway (expressway) runs from Biarritz (France) to Burgos. From there, take the N1 to Madrid and continue on the E4 via Badajoz and Setúbal, or the E4 to Mérida and then go via the E102 through Seville. The distance from Calais to the Algarve is over 2,000 km (1,300 miles), you might consider the long-distance car ferry service from Plymouth to Santander in northern Spain (a 24-hour trip). From Santander, follow the N611 to the E3 via Valladolid and Coimbra.

By Rail. Portugal is linked to the European railway network; connections to Lisbon are possible from points throughout Spain, France, and the rest of continental Europe. Travel to Portugal is included on any InterRail or EurailPass; the Eurodomino pass is available for travel within Portugal only for a 3-, 5- or 10-day period, but may not be as good a deal as it is on more expensive rail networks in northern Europe.

The Portuguese national railway network is called **Caminhos de Ferro Portugueses** (Tel. 800/200 904, 21/888 40 25, or 21/811 20 00; <www.cp.pt>). The Santa Apolónia station in Lisbon (Avenida Dom Henrique; Tel. 21/888 40 25) serves all international trains. Daily international trains run between Paris and Lisbon (Sud Express), crossing the frontier at Vilar Formoso; between Lisbon and Madrid, crossing the frontier at Marvão; and between Porto and Vigo, crossing the frontier at Valença. Connecting trains to the Algarve depart from Lisbon's Terreiro do Paço via Barreiro.

By Sea. Lisbon is a major port, and several cruise ships include a port-of-call in the capital, including Celebrity, Renaissance, Princess, Norwegian, and Royal Caribbean. Ferries from Great Britain (Brittany Ferries) go to Santander, Spain from Plymouth and Portsmouth, and to Bilbao, Spain from Portsmouth (P & O Ferries). Crossings range from 24 to 36 hours. The drive from northern Spain to the Algarve is then likely to take another 15 to 18 hours.

GUIDES AND TOURS *(guias; visitas guiadas)*
Information on half- or full-day city tours is available from tourist information offices (see page 169) or travel agents.

Portugal

All the excursion firms, such as **Portugal Tours** (Tel. 21/351 12 20), offer trips to Mafra, Queluz, Sintra, Cascais, and Estoril, as well as a long day's outing covering major sites north of Lisbon: Fátima, Alcobaça and Batalha, Óbidos, and Nazaré. If you are traveling independently, you can cover all these at greater leisure, also making an overnight stop or two on the way.

We'd like an English-speaking guide.	**Queremos um guia que fale inglês.**

H

HEALTH and MEDICAL CARE (See also EMERGENCIES)

Standards of hygiene are generally very high; the most likely illness to befall travelers will be due to an excess of sun or alcohol. The water is safe to drink, but bottled water is always safest, and is available everywhere. Even most local people drink bottled water, *agua com gas* (carbonated) or *sem gas* (still). It is good, clean, and inexpensive.

Farmácias (drugstores/chemists) are open during normal business hours. At other times one shop in each neighborhood is on duty around the clock. Addresses are listed in newspapers. To locate night pharmacies, call Tel. 118.

For more serious illness or injury, the **British Hospital** (Rua Saraiva de Carvalho, 49, Lisbon; Tel. 21/395 5 67) has English-speaking staff.

Medical insurance to cover illness or accident while abroad is a good investment. EU nationals with EU form E111 obtained well before departure get free emergency treatment at Social Security and Municipal hospitals in Portugal. Privately billed hospital visits are expensive.

Where's the nearest pharmacy?	**Aónde é a farmácia (de guardia) mais perto?**
I need a doctor/dentist.	**Preciso de um médico/dentista.**
an ambulance	**uma ambulância**
hospital	**hospital**
an upset stomach	**mal de estômago**
sunstroke	**uma insolação**
a fever	**febre**

HOLIDAYS (*feriado*)
National holidays:

1 Jan	*Ano Novo*	New Year's Day
25 April	*Dia da Liberdade*	Liberty Day
1 May	*Festa do Trabalho*	Labor Day
10 June	*Dia de Portugal*	National Day
15 Aug	*Assunção*	Assumption
5 October	*Heróis da República*	Republic Day
1 November	*Todos-os-Santos*	All Saints' Day
1 December	*Dia da Independência*	Independence Day
8 December	*Imaculada Conceição*	Immaculate Conception
25 December	*Natal*	Christmas Day
Movable dates:	*Carnaval*	Shrove Tuesday
	Sexta-feira Santa	Good Friday
	Corpo de Deus	Corpus Christi

In addition, every town closes down and takes to the streets at least once a year in honor of its own patron saint. See the Calendar of Events on page 136 for other events.

Are you open tomorrow?	**Estão abertos amanhã?**
When do you close?	**Quándo fecha?**

L

LANGUAGE

Portuguese, a derivative of Latin, is spoken in such far-flung spots as Brazil, Angola, Mozambique, and Macau—former colonies of Portugal. Your high-school Spanish may help with signs and menus, but will not unlock the mysteries of spoken Portuguese. The Portuguese in Portugal is much more closed and gutteral-sounding, and is also spoken much faster, than in Brazil.

Almost everyone understands Spanish and many speak French. A surprising number of people in Lisbon speak quite passable if not wholly fluent English. Schoolchildren are taught French and English, as well as Portuguese.

The *Berlitz Portuguese Phrasebook and Dictionary* covers most situations you're likely to encounter during a visit to Portugal. Also useful is the *Berlitz Portuguese-English/English-Portuguese Pocket Dictionary,* containing a special menu-reader supplement.

Portugal

Here are some useful phrases to get you going (see the front cover flap of this guide):

Good evening	**Boa noite**
Goodbye	**Adeus**
excuse me/you're welcome	**perdão/de nada**
please	**faz favor**
where/when/how	**onde/quando/como**
yesterday/today/tomorrow	**ontem/hoje/amanhã**
day/week/month/year	**dia/semana/mês/ano**
left/right	**esquerdo/direito**
good/bad	**bom/mau**
big/small	**grande/pequeno**
cheap/expensive	**barato/caro**
hot/cold	**quente/frio**
old/new	**velho/novo**
open/closed	**aberto/fechado**
Please write it down.	**Escreva-lo, por favor.**
What does this mean?	**Que quer dizer isto?**
Help me, please.	**Ajude-me, por favor.**
Just a minute.	**Um momento.**
Get a doctor quickly.	**Chame um médico, depressa.**
What time is it?	**Que hora tem/é?**

DAYS

Sunday	**domingo**
Monday	**segunda-feira**
Tuesday	**terça-feira**
Wednesday	**quarta-feira**
Thursday	**quinta-feira**
Friday	**sexta-feira**
Saturday	**sábado**
What day is it today?	**Que dia é hoje?**

M

MAPS (*um mapa*)

The tourist information offices in most towns are well-stocked with maps sufficient for most purposes. The red, green, and yellow

"Portugal Touristic Map" available at some tourist information offices covers the entire country.

MEDIA (*jornal; revista*)

Europe's principal newspapers, including most British dailies and the *International Herald Tribune*, edited in Paris, are available on the day of publication at many newsstands and hotels. Popular foreign magazines are also sold at the same shops or stands. The most important Portuguese-language daily is *Diário de Notîcias*, which contains full cultural listings.

Four television channels are widely available in Portugal: two are government-run and two are independent. Films are usually shown in the original language with subtitles. Most hotels at the four-star level and above have access to satellite reception that gets Sky, CNN, and others.

Do you have any English-language newspapers?	**Tem jornais em inglês?**

MONEY (*dinheiro*)

Currency (*moeda*). In common with most other European countries, the euro (EUR) is the official currency used in Portugal. Notes are denominated in 5, 10, 20, 50, 100 and 500 euros; coins in 1 and 2 euros and 1, 2, 5, 10, 20 and 50 cents.

Currency Exchange (*banco; câmbio*). Normal banking hours are Mon-Fri 8:30am-3pm. In tourist areas, some banks remain open later and on weekends to change money, and there is a 24-hour exchange office at the airport. The exchange office at Santa Apolónia railway station is open 8:30am-8:30pm and one bank in Praça dos Restauradores is open 6-11pm for the benefit of tourists. A substantial flat rate fee is charged for changing travelers' checks; you will need to show your passport. Automatic money-exchanging machines (ATMs) are much the easiest method of obtaining euros and they provide by far the best exchange rates.

Portugal

ATMs *(caixa automática)*. Automatic teller machines outside banks, identified by the MB (MultiBanco) sign, are widely available. From them you can draw funds in euros against your bank/credit card account with a Visa or Mastercard, or other debit card on one of the international networks like Cirrus or Plus, provided you know the personal identification number (PIN). The PIN number should be four digits.

Credit Cards *(cartão de crédito)*. Standard international credit cards are widely accepted in Portugal. In some shops and restaurants, especially in small towns outside Lisbon, however, you may not be able to use a credit card.

Travelers' Checks. Less necessary now that ATMs have proliferated across the world, international travelers' checks (such as Thomas Cooke or American Express) can be cashed at any bank.

Can I pay with this credit card?	**Posso pagar com cartão de crédito?**
I want to change some pounds/dollars.	**Queria trocar libras/dólares.**
Can you cash a travelers' cheque?	**Pode pagar um cheque de viagem?**

 O

OPEN HOURS *(horas de abertura)*
Most shops and offices are open 9am-1pm and 3-7pm weekdays, and 9am-1pm Saturday. Most museums are closed on Mondays and public holidays (the tourist office has a full list of those open on Monday); palaces are closed on either Mondays or Tuesdays. On every other day (including Sunday) they are open 10 or 11am–5pm, but most close from noon–2pm or 1–2:30pm. A number of shopping malls in the larger cities are open from 10am–10pm or even midnight, including Sunday.

P

POLICE (*polícia*) (See also EMERGENCIES on page 157)
Police wearing armbands marked CD (it stands for *Corpo Distrital*, meaning local corps) are assigned to assist tourists and normally speak at least a smidgen of a foreign language. On highways, traffic is controlled by the Guarda Nacional Republicana (GNR) in white cars or on motorcycles. For a general emergency, dial Tel. 112.

Where's the nearest police station?	**Onde fica o posto de policia mais próximo?**
Police officer	**Senhor Guarda**

POST OFFICES (*correios*)
Post offices are indicated by the letters CTT (*Correios, Telegrafos e Telefones*). The mail service is generally good, though it can get bogged down during the height of the season. You can buy stamps from most shops as well — they usually display a sign that says *Correios*. Most mailboxes follow the British pillar-box design and are painted bright red.

Main offices are open 8:30am to 6:30 or 7pm Monday-Friday; local branches are open 9am to 12:30pm and 2 to 6pm Monday-Friday. Main post offices in major cities are open on Saturday mornings as well.

A postcard or letter under 20 g. anywhere in the EU costs €0.52; to the rest of the world, €0.61. Mail may take up to a week to reach a European destination. There is also a 3-day "Azul" (express) service.

Where's the nearest post office?	**Onde fica a estação de correios mais próxima?**
A stamp for this letter/ postcard, please.	**Um selo para esta carta/este postal, por favor.**
express (special delivery)	**expresso**
airmail	**via aérea**
registered	**registado**

PUBLIC TRANSPORTATION (*transporte*)
Public transport generally runs from around 6am or 7am to midnight or 1am.

Portugal

Local buses (*autocarros*) and **trams** (*eléctricos*). Bus and tram stops in cities usually have a small route map and an indication of which buses stop there. You can buy your ticket on the bus, or you can buy passes or blocks of tickets from kiosks and some shops (if in doubt, ask at the tourist office).

Underground (*Metro*). Lisbon has two lines, providing a fast way of getting around, though there is a limited number of stops.

Taxis. Most taxis are black with a green roof and a "taxi" sign. City taxis have meters, but are entitled to charge an extra 20% at night and an extra sum for each item of luggage. Tip about 10%. If there is no meter, it is essential to establish a price before your trip starts. Most taxis use taxi stands, but some cruise the streets looking for passengers.

Intercity buses. Intercity buses are a fairly fast, comfortable, and cheap way of getting around Portugal. The majority of buses are operated by RN (Rodoviária Nacional), except in the Minho and Trás-os-Montes areas, where there is a profusion of different companies. Buses are likely to operate out of the same central bus station, though in cities there can be several stations, in which case it is worth asking for advice at the tourist office. The bus network is far more extensive than the train system.

Trains (*comboio*). Trains are operated by CP (Caminhos de Ferro Portugueses), the national rail company. Many lines have closed in recent years, to be replaced by buses. Regional trains stop at most stations, intercity trains cost more and make fewer stops, while express (*Rápido*) trains run from Lisbon to Porto non-stop and cost still more. Direct service from Porto and Lisbon to the Algarve are available on the *Comboio Azul* (the "Blue Train").

All trains have first- and second-class cars. Tickets cost less on "Blue Days" (*Dias Azuis*), which usually occur in the middle of the week. Discounts of 50% are available for senior citizens (though you first need to get a free Cartão Dourada) on trains running from 6:30am to 9:30am, and from 5pm to 8pm, except at weekends and on public holidays, and on suburban trains. As a rule, prices are lower than in most western European countries. *Bilhete Turísticos* offer unlimited train travel for 7, 14, or 21 days. Inter-rail, Inter-rail 26 plus, Rail Europe Senior and Eurail passes are all valid in Portugal.

Lisbon is the central hub of the train network. There are four stations: Santa Apolónia for international services and to northern Portugal; Cais do Sodré for commuter trains to the western suburbs, and to Estoril and Cascais; Rossio for Sintra and the west; and Sul e Sueste for the south (including the Algarve) and the southeast (ticket prices will include the ferry trip across the Tagus, if necessary).

Ferries (*barcaça*). Many boats offer services across the Tagus, up various rivers, such as the Douro and the Guadiana, to the Tróia Peninsula and to the offshore islands. Ask at local tourist offices for further details.

Domestic Flights. TAP (Air Portugal) flies between Lisbon, Porto and Faro. TAP also flies from Lisbon to Madeira and the Azores.

Where can I get a taxi?	**Onde posso encontrar um táxi?**
What's the fare to…?	**Quanto custa o percurso para…?**
Where is the nearest railway station/bus stop?	**Onde é a estação ferroviária/ a paragem de autocarros mais próxima?**
When's the next bus/train to…?	**Quando parte o próximo autocarro/comboio para…?**
I want a ticket to…	**Queria um bilhete para…**
one-way (single)	**ida**
round-trip (return)	**ida e volta**
first/second class	**primeira/segunda classe**
Will you tell me when to get off?	**Pode dizer-me quando devo descer?**
Can you give us a lift to...?	**Pode levar-nos a...?**

R

RELIGION

The Portuguese are predominantly Roman Catholic, a fact reflected in surviving religious rituals and saints' days that are public holidays. The tourist information office has a list of services for English-speaking Catholics and other worshipers.

The shrine at Fátima, recently visited by Pope John Paul II, is one of the most important pilgrimages in Catholicism.

T

TELEPHONES (*telefones*)

Portugal's country code is 351. The local area code must be dialed before all phone numbers, even for local calls (9-digit total).

White Portugal Telecom public telephones that accept both coins and prepaid telephone cards are found throughout the Portugal's villages, towns and cities. Coin boxes take a variety of euro coins; unused coins are returned. *Credifone* telephone cards can be purchased at post offices.

Local, national, and international calls can also be made from hotels, but usually with an exorbitant surcharge. Make these with an international calling card, if you must make them from your hotel room. Visitors from the US and Canada are advised to get the international access code in Portugal for their long distance telephone carrier at home before departure.

To make an international call, dial 00 for an international line (both Europe and overseas; eg UK 0044, USA 001) + the country code + phone number (including the area code, without the initial '0', where there is one).

If you wish to send a fax, you may do so from most hotels, though the charge may seem particularly high.

reverse-charge call	**paga pelo destinatário**
Can you get me this number in …?	**Pode ligar-me para este número em …?**
I want to send a telegram to …	**Quero mandar um telegrama para …**

TIME ZONES (*hora local*)

In 1992 Portugal switched time zones to align it with most of the European Union. Now it is at GMT + 1 in winter, making sunrise rather late. From the last Sunday in March until the last Sunday in October, the clocks are moved one hour ahead for summer time, GMT + 2. In summer the chart looks like this:

New York	London	Paris	**Lisbon**	Sydney	Auckland
6am	11am	noon	**noon**	8pm	10pm

TIPPING (*serviço; gorjeta*)

Hotel and restaurant bills are generally all-inclusive, but an additional tip of 5-10% is common and even expected in restaurants. Hotel porters, per bag, generally receive €0.50. Taxi drivers do not normally expect a tip, though one should be given for any special services or information rendered.

TOILETS/RESTROOMS (*lavabo; casa de banho; serviços*)

Public toilets exist in some large towns, but almost every bar and restaurant has one available for public use. While it's polite to buy a coffee or drink if you drop in to use their restroom, no one will yell at you for not doing so.

Where are the toilets? **Onde é a casa de banho?**

TOURIST INFORMATION (*informação turística*)

Portuguese National Tourist Offices (ICEP, or Investimentos, Comércio e Turismo de Portugal) are maintained in many countries:

Canada: Suite 1005, 60 Bloor Street West, Toronto, Ont. M4W 3B8; Tel. (416) 921 7376.

Ireland: 54 Dawson Street, Dublin. Tel. (353) 670 9133.

South Africa: 4th floor, Sunnyside Ridge, Sunnyside Drive. PO Box 2473 Houghton, Johannesburg. Tel. (2711) 484 3487.

United Kingdom: 22/25a Sackville St, London W1X 1DE; Tel. (020) 7494 1441.

USA: 590 Fifth Ave, 4th floor, New York, NY 10036; Tel. (212) 354 4403.

In Lisbon, the main tourism information office is in Palácio Foz, on Praça dos Restauradores; Tel. 21/346 36 43. There is another office at the airport (Arrivals terminal).

A recently inaugurated **help line** for tourist information, the *linha verde turista,* is Tel. 080/296 296. The free service, in Portuguese, English, French and Spanish, is available from 9am-midnight Mon-Sat and 9am-8pm Sundays and holidays. Information on sights, hotels, restaurants, transportation, hospitals and police is available.

Virtually every town has a local tourist office (*Turismo*).

Where is the tourist office? **Onde é o turismo?**

Portugal

WEB SITES AND INTERNET CAFÉS *(cafés cibernéticos)*

Before you leave on your trip to Portugal:

Check <www.pousadas.pt> for information about government-run accommodations.

General country information and a tourism database can be found at <www.portugalvirtual.pt>. There are links to accommodations.

The official Web site of the Portuguese Tourism office is <www.portugal.org>.

The Portuguese national airline (Tap/Air Portugal) has a site at <www.tap.pt>.

For timetables and information on international and domestic trains, visit the site of the national railway network, Caminhos de Ferro Portugueses, at <www.cp.pt>.

The tourist information offices in Lisbon and Porto have lists of Internet (cyber) cafés where travelers can go to check e-mail for a reasonable hourly (or partial-hour) fee. Outside the major towns and tourist resorts in the Algarve, Internet cafés are more difficult to come by.

WEIGHTS AND MEASURES (For fuel and distance charts see DRIVING IN PORTUGAL)

Length

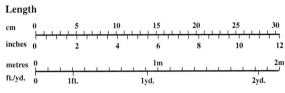

Weight

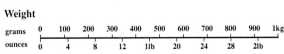

Temperature

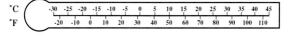

The metric system is used in Portugal.

 Y

YOUTH HOSTELS (*pousadas de juventude*)
There are 18 hostels spread across the country, many of which serve meals. It is best to join the International Youth Hostel Federation before you depart, but you can join up on arrival as a junior member (14 to 21 years old) or a senior (22 to 40); headquarters of the Portuguese Youth Hostel Association (Associação Portuguesa de Pousadas de Juventude), Avenida Duque de Ávila 137, 1000 Lisbon; Tel. 21/355 90 81.

More Useful Expressions

here/there	**aqui/ali**
free (vacant)/occupied	**livre/ocupado**
early/late	**cedo/tarde**
easy/difficult	**fácil/difícil**
Is there an admission charge?	**Paga-se entrada?**

Recommended Hotels

Hotel prices are fairly reasonable across Portugal, though in Lisbon they have risen in recent years to match most Western European destinations, even surpassing popular cities like Barcelona at the top levels.

   Room price guidelines below are rack rates for a double room with bath in high season (generally April–October), including breakfast and VAT (value-added tax, currently 5% of room price). All hotels except for the smallest residential inns accept major credit cards. For making reservations, Portugal's country telephone code is 351.

€€€€€	over 200 euros
€€€€	150–200 euros
€€€	100–150 euros
€€	60–100 euros
€	below 60 euros

LISBON

As Janelas Verdes €€€–€€€€ *Rua das Janelas Verdes, 47; Tel. 21-396 81 43; fax 21-396 81 44; <www.heritage.pt>*. A charming and elegant hotel in the sophisticated Lapa district, near the River Tagus and Museu de Arte Antiga. This small hotel occupies the 18th-century townhouse of one of Portugal's most famous writers, Eço de Queirós, and has recently expanded into the home next door. Has a quiet, garden-like courtyard and top-floor library, and some rooms have superb views of the river. Wheelchair access. 29 rooms.

Hotel Apartamento Orion Eden €€ *Praça dos Restauradores, 24; Tel; 21-321 66 00; fax 21-321 66 66; e-mail <eden.lisboa@ mail.telepac.pt>*. In a famous Art Deco building right on Praça dos Restauradores, this modern apartment-hotel is a great deal, especially for families. There are kitchen-equipped studios and full apartments, with daily or weekly maid service. Panoramic pool and breakfast service. Wheelchair access. 134 rooms.

Hotel Avenida Palace €€€€ *Rua 1 de Dezembro, 123. Tel. 21/346 01 51; fax 21/342 28 84; <www.hotel-avenida-palace.pt>*. Right on Rossio, the major plaza in the Baixa district, the recently remodeled Avenida Palace is one of Lisbon's finest luxury hotels. Magnificent Old World feel. Disabled access. 82 rooms.

Hotel Britania €€€ *Rua Rodrigues Sampaio, 17. Tel. 21/315 50 16; fax 21/315 50 21; <www.heritage.pt>*. A 1940s townhouse with spacious, elegantly appointed bedrooms. Lovingly restored with lovely Art Deco and clubby touches. Disabled access. 30 rooms.

Hotel Metropole €€€ *Rua 1 de Dezembro, 123. Tel. 21/346 01 51; fax 21/342 28 84; e-mail <almeida_hotels@ip.pt>*. One of Lisbon's best deals is this classic, Art Deco 1920s hotel in the heart of the Baixa. Large rooms with period antiques. Disabled access. 36 rooms.

Lapa Palace €€€€€ *Rua Pau da Bandeira, 4. Tel. 21/395 00 05; fax 395 06 65; <www.orient-expresshotels.com>*. Loving conversion of a palatial old mansion overlooking the River Tagus in Lapa. Landscaped gardens and outdoor pool. Plush rooms. Disabled access. 102 rooms.

Lisboa Regency Chiado €€€ *Rua Nova do Almada, 114. Tel. 21/325 61 00; fax 21/325 61 61; e-mail <regencychiado@madeiraregency.pt>*. Lisbon's newest hotel, in the heart of the Chiado district. Chic lobby and rooms. Disabled access. 40 rooms.

York House €€€€ *Rua das Janelas Verdes 32. Tel. 21/396 27 85; fax 21/397 27 93; e-mail <yorkhouse@mail.telepac.pt>*. Converted 17th-century convent near the Museum of Ancient Art. Elegant rooms. Recommended restaurant. Disabled access. 34 rooms.

ESTORIL COAST

Hotel Albatroz €€€€–€€€€€ *Rua Frederico Arouca 100, 2750 Cascais. Tel. 21/484 73 80; fax 21/484 48 27; <www.albatrozhotel.pt>.* Cascais's most elegant hotel is this mansion perched above the Praia da Rainha beach. Public rooms and accommodations are very luxurious. Outdoor pool and lovely gardens. Nice restaurant. Disabled access. 46 rooms.

Hotel do Guincho €€€€ *Praia do Guincho, 2750 Cascais. Tel. 21/487 04 91; fax 21/487 04 31.* Former 16th-century fortress perched on a rocky ledge overlooking Guincho beach. Marvelous antique touches throughout. Most rooms have fireplaces, many balconies with views of the sea. 36 rooms.

NEAR LISBON

Quinta da Capela €€€ *Estrada Velha de Colares, 2710 Sintra. Tel. 21/929 01 70; fax 21/929 34 25.* A rambling 16th-century house on an old country estate outside Sintra. Gorgeous grounds. Closed November–March (cottages open year-round). 11 rooms.

Pousada de São Filipe €€€ *Castelo de São Filipe, 2900 Setúbal; Tel. 265/ 52 38 44; fax 265/53 25 38; <www.pousadas.pt>.* Luxury pousada inside the walls of a fortress built in 1590, overlooking the port of Setúbal. Great views. Close to the Serra de Arrábida National Park. 14 rooms.

RIBATEJO & ESTEMADURA

Pousada do Castelo €€€€ *Paço Real, 2510 Óbidos. Tel. 262/95 91 05; fax 262/95 91 48; <www.pousadas.pt>.* In-demand pousada in Portugal fashioned from an historic monument, the medieval castle inside the walled town. Stunning views and celebrated restaurant. A couple of two-story suites are in castle towers. Reserve well in advance. 9 rooms.

Quinta do Campo €€ *Valado dos Frades, 2450 Nazaré. Tel. 262/57 71 35;fax 262/57 75 55;<www.maisturismo.pt/qtcampo>.* Family-run, charming 600-year-old manor house, 5 km (3 miles) from Nazaré. Swimming pool, tennis court, and gardens. 8 rooms.

Hotel dos Templários €€ *Largo Cândido dos Reis, 1, 2300 Tomar. Tel. 492/32 17 30; fax 249/32 21 91.* A large hotel on the banks of the river. Large, standard rooms and spacious lobby. Indoor swimming pool and tennis court, health club. Disabled access. 176 rooms.

THE BEIRAS

Quinta das Lágrimas. €€€ *Santa Clara, 3041 Coimbra. Tel. 239/80 23 80; fax. 239/44 16 95;<www.supernet.pt/ hotelagrimas>* A Relais & Chateaux property; an 18th-century palace on 4 hectares (10 acres) of gardens and woods across the river from old Coimbra. Handsomely decorated rooms, excellent restaurant (see page 183), large pool, and golf driving range. 39 rooms.

Palace Hotel do Buçaco €€€€ *Buçaco Forest, 3050 Luso. Tel. 231/93 01 01; fax 231/93 05 09; e-mail <bussacopalace@ clix.pt>.* Splendidly ornate and palatial hotel, built as a hunting retreat for the last kings of Portugal. In the legendary Buçaco forest. 60 rooms.

Casa das Tílias. €€ *São Romão, 6270 Seia. Tel. 238/39 00 55; fax 238/39 01 23; <www.tílias.com>.* A charming early 19th-century country estate in the Serra da Estrela. Friendly family atmosphere, downstairs pub. "Mercury" suite is huge. 6 rooms.

PORTO AND THE DOURO VALLEY

Hotel da Bolsa €€ *Rua Ferreira Borges 101, 4050 Porto; Tel. 222/026 768/69/70; fax 222 058 888; e-mail <hoteldabolsa @mail.telepac.pt>.* Older-style hotel in central Porto located adjacent to the Stock Exchange. Rooms are comfortable and nicely furnished. Good value. Disabled access. 36 rooms.

Porto Carlton Hotel €€€ *Praça da Ribeira, 1 Porto; Tel. 223/402 300; fax 223/402 400; <www.pestana.com>.* A new, small hotel ideally located in Ribeira, right on the waterfront. Rooms are sleekly modern, large, and comfortable. Many have superb views of Dom Luís bridge and river. Disabled access. 48 rooms.

Hotel Infante de Sagres €€€€ *Praça D. Filipa de Lencastre, 62, 4050 Porto. Tel. 223/398 500; fax 223/398 599; <www.hotelinfantesagres.pt>.* Luxury hotel in downtown Porto. Though it seems like it's from an earlier age, it was actually built in 1951. Good service and handsome public rooms, nice restaurant. Disabled access. 74 rooms.

Pousada Solar da Rede €€€–€€€€ *Santa Cristina, 5040 Mesão Frio. Tel. 254/89 01 30; fax 254/89 01 39; <www.pousadas.pt>.* With stunning views over the River Douro, this gracious 18th-century manor house has orchards and a 27-hectare (67 acre) vineyard. Regal furnishings and public rooms. Swimming pool, tennis court. 31 rooms.

Vintage House €€€ *Lugar da Ponte, 5085 Pinhão. Tel. 254/73 02 30.; fax 254/73 02 38; <www. maisturismo.pt/1/1475>.* Lovely hotel owned by Taylor-Fonseca, one of the major port wine producers, with luxurious traditional styling, superb restaurant, and library bar. Tennis court, swimming pool. Disabled access. 43 rooms.

THE MINHO

Pousada de Santa Marinha €€€–€€€€ *Costa, 4800 Guimarães; Tel. 253/51 44 53/4/5; fax 253/51 44 59; <www.pousadas.pt>.* A stunningly converted 12th-century monastery in the Penha hills 3 km (2 miles) from Guimarães. Beautiful antiques and art, spectacular cloister and gardens, great views of Guimarães. 49 rooms.

Castelo do Bom Jesus €€ *4710 Braga. Tel. 253/281 322; fax 253/679 202; <www.maisturismo.pt/bomjesus.html>.* Secluded 18th-century seignorial house estate on 3 hectares (8 acres) of gardens with waterfalls, pools, gazebos, and grottos. In the same family for 250 years. Terrific hilltop views. Large pool, tennis court. 13 rooms.

Pousada Santa Maria do Bouro €€€–€€€€ *4720-688 Amares. Tel. 253/37 19 71/2/3; fax 253/37 19 76; <www.pousadas.pt>.* Daring modern adaptation of a former Cistercian Monastery between Braga and the Gerês mountain range. Sleek furnishings, exposed medieval stone walls. Beautiful bar and dining room. Disabled access. 30 rooms.

Pousada do Monte de Santa Luzia Hotel €€€ *Santa Luzia, 4900 Viana do Castelo; Tel. 258/82 88 90/1; fax 258/82 88 92; <www.pousadas.pt>.* Peaceful 1930s hotel perched on a hill overlooking the resort town of Viana, River Lima, and the Atlantic. Tennis court, secluded swimming pool, gardens. 47 rooms.

Quinta do Paço de Calheiros €€ *Calheiros, 4990 Ponte de Lima; Tel. 258/94 71 64; fax 258/94 72 94.* Sumptuous rural inn in terraced fields above the river, 7 km (4 miles) from Ponte de Lima. Rooms and apartments are beautifully furnished. Horseback riding, tennis, and swimming pool. 10 rooms.

TRÁS-OS-MONTES

Forte de São Francisco €€€ *5400 Chaves. Tel. 276/33 37 00; fax 276/33 37 01; <www.forte-s-francisco-hoteis.pt>.* Marvelously converted 16th-century convent within the Fortress of São Francisco, with large rooms, handsome furnishings and details. Excellent restaurant and tavern for informal meals. Tennis court, sauna. Disabled access. 58 rooms.

Pousada de São Bartolomeu €€ *5300 Bragança; Tel. 273/33 14 93; fax 273/234 53.* Comfortable modern pousada on a hill overlooking the Bragança citadel. Large rooms have nice terraces. Disabled access. 28 rooms.

ALENTEJO

Pousada de Vila Viçosa (Dom João IV). €€€–€€€€
7160 Terreiro do Paço, 7160 Vila Viçosa. Tel. 268/980 742/5; fax: 268/980 747; <www.pousadas.pt>. Located right next door to the royal palace of the Dukes of Bragança in what was formerly a 16th-century convent. Traditional style, with large rooms and central courtyard. Swimming pool. Disabled access. 36 rooms.

Pousada dos Lóios. €€€€ *Largo Conde de Vila Flor, 7000 Évora. Tel. 266/240 51/2; fax 266/272 48; <www.pousadas.pt>.* A luxurious 15th-century convent next to the Roman Temple. Antique furnishings and Manueline stone arches. Chic restaurant, outdoor pool. 32 rooms.

Pousada de Rainha Santa Isabel. €€€€ *Largo D. Dinis 7100 Estremoz. Tel. 268/33 20 75; fax: 268/33 20 79; <www.pousadas.pt>.* Estremoz castle (which King D. Dinis built for his Queen, Santa Isabel) with museum-quality furnishings, gardens, and swimming pool enclosed by ramparts. Restaurant hosts special royal banquets, with staff in period costume. 31 rooms.

Hotel Convento de São Paulo €€€€ *Aldeia da Serra 7170 Redondo. Tel. 266/98 91 60; fax 266/99 91 04; <www.maisturismo.pt/hspaulo>.* Convent dating to 1128 between Estremoz and Évora on the slopes of the D'Ossa mountains, among 600 hectares (1,483 acres) of woodlands and gardens. Long corridors are lined with 50,000 azulejo tiles. Excellent restaurant with vaulted ceilings and 18th-century frescoes. 29 rooms.

Pousada Flor da Rosa €€€–€€€€ *7430 Crato. Tel. 245/99 72 10/1; fax 245/99 72 12; <www.pousadas.pt>.* Architectural showpiece, a starkly modern conversion of a ruined 14th-century castle and convent. Sleek furnishings and brilliant use of space. Large rooms and beautiful pool. Disabled access. 25 rooms.

THE ALGARVE

Hotel de Lagos €€€€ *Rua Nova da Aldeia, 8600 Lagos; Tel. 282/76 99 67; fax 282/76 99 20; e-mail <hotel.lagos@mail.telepac.pt>.* Hotel with character and style in old Lagos. Attractive poolside areas, indoor swimming pool, fitness center, tennis courts. Disabled access. 319 rooms.

Hotel Bela Vista €€€ *Avenida Tomás Cabreira, Praia da Rocha, 8500 Portimão; Tel. 282/45 04 80; fax 282/41 53 69.* The first hotel in the Algarve, a mansion overlooking the beach. Resembling a church more than a hotel, it was built as a summer house in 1916. 14 rooms.

Pestana Carlton Alvor Hotel €€€€€ *Praia de Três Irmãos, 8501 Alvor; Tel. 282/40 09 00; fax 282/40 09 99; e-mail <pestana.hotels@mail.telepac.pt>.* Large and luxurious hotel among thick trees and gardens on cliffs, overlooking fine beaches. Olympic-size saltwater pool with ocean views. Three restaurants with terraces and different cuisines. Tennis courts, full spa. Disabled access. 198 rooms.

Estalagem Abrigo da Montanha €€–€€€ *Estrada Monchique-Fóia, 8550 Monchique. Tel. 282/91 21 31; fax 282/91 36 60; e-mail <abrigodamontanha@hotmail.com>.* High up in the Serra de Monchique, a wood-and-granite mountain lodge retreat. Pretty rooftop pool and café-restaurant across the road. 16 rooms.

Vila Joya €€€€ *Praia da Galé, 8200 Albufeira; Tel. 289/59 17 95; fax 289/59 12 01; <www.harras.be/alfagar>.* Very stylish Moorish-influenced villa just minutes from calm Galé beach. Beautiful public rooms. Most rooms have sea views. Reserve several months in advance. 17 rooms.

Hotel Quinta do Lago €€€€€ *Quinta do Lago, 8135 Almancil; Tel. 289/35 03 50; fax 289/39 63 93; <www.quintadolagohotel.com>.* Standard-bearer for luxury and leisure situated in 2,000 acres of gardens and woods. Three golf courses along with Ria Formosa Nature Preserve. Water sports, health club, pools, and beach. Disabled access. 141 rooms.

Convento de São António €€ *Atalaia 56, 8800 Tavira; Tel./fax 281/32 56 32.* This small, family-owned guesthouse was a monastery in the 17th century. Nice swimming pool and central patio. Minimum stay required. 7 rooms.

Residencial Praia do Vau €€ *Apartado 158, 8501 Portimão; Tel. 282/401 312; fax 282/401 756.* A small, rustic, comfortable inn in an attractive Algarvian house just 200 m (219 yards) from the Praia do Vau beach (west of Praia da Rocha). 21 rooms.

Sheraton Algarve (Pine Cliffs) Hotel & Resort €€€€€ *Praia da Falésia, 8200 Albufeira; Tel. 289/500 100 (toll-free in UK 800/325 454 545; in US, 800/325 3535); fax 289/501 950; <www. luxurycollection.com>.* One of the Algarve's most distinguished and luxurious developments, surrounded by pines at the top of dramatic cliffs. Handsome Moorish styling, excellent restaurants, and extensive sporting facilities, including 9-hole cliff-top golf course, tennis, semi-private beach, 3 pools and spa. Brand-new luxury "Golf Suites," plus villas and apartments. Great facilities for children. Disabled access. 215 rooms (33 suites, 70 apartments).

Vila Channa €€€ *São Rafael, 8200 Albufeira; Tel. 289/592 354; fax 289/591 597.* A nice, clean, villa-style small hotel a short walk from a couple of the prettiest beaches near Albufeira, Castelo and São Rafael. Nice pool. 18 rooms.

Recommended Restaurants

Even the top restaurants are fairly affordable by the standards of European capitals. The "tourist menu" (*ementa turística*) in many restaurants, especially at lunchtime, can be an excellent value at 7.50–12.50 euros, with either wine, beer, mineral water, or a soft drink included.

The prices indicated are for starter, main course, and dessert, with wine, per person. (Note that some fish or shellfish dishes will be more expensive.) Service and VAT of 12% are included in the bill.

Many restaurants close for the entire month of August. Unless noted below, all restaurants accept major credit cards.

In addition to those listed below, check the hotel listings for hotels with recommended restaurants. Pousadas are almost always good bets for regional cuisine. The most impressive pousada restaurants are included below.

€€€€	over 40 euros
€€€	25–40 euros
€€	15–25 euros
€	below 15 euros

LISBON

Cervejeria da Trindade *€–€€ Rua Nova da Trindade 20 (Bairro Alto). Tel. 21/346 08 08.* Open daily for lunch and dinner (until late). A famous old beer hall and restaurant in a former monastery. Popular Portuguese cooking and seafood specialties at good prices.

Pap d'Açorda *€€–€€€ Rua da Atalaia 5-597 (Bairro Alto). Tel. 21/346 48 11.* Open Tues–Sat for lunch and dinner; Mon, dinner only. One of Lisbon's hippest spots, cool but informal. Traditional and creative Portuguese dishes like açorda real thick shellfish stew with lobster and shrimp).

Portugal

Tavares €€€–€€€€ *Rua da Misericórdia 37 (Bairro Alto). Tel. 21/342 11 12.* Open Mon–Fri for lunch and dinner; Sun, dinner only. A stylish and immensely popular restaurant-café with ornate ceilings, mirrors, and chandeliers. Serving classical French cuisine for more than a century.

Bico do Sapato €€€ *Avenida Infante D. Henrique (Cais da Pedra, Baixa). Tel. 21/881 03 20.* Open daily for lunch and dinner. New and trendy restaurant across from Santa Apolónia station. Excellent and fairly priced creative Portuguese menu, good list of local wines.

Gambrinus €€€€ *Rua das Portas de Santo Antão 25 (Baixa). Tel. 21/342 14 66.* Open daily for lunch and dinner (until late). Sophisticated restaurant near Rossio. Specializes in traditional Portuguese and Galician dishes, which means fresh seafood.

Doca de Santo Amaro €€€–€€€€ *Alcântara Mar (waterfront).* Most open daily for lunch and dinner. Lively bar-and-restaurant scene in renovated warehouses along the river docks, near the 25 de Abril bridge and Belém. Stroll along the dock and choose a restaurant that looks appealing.

São Jerónimo €€ *Rua dos Jerónimos, 12 (Belem). Tel. 21/364 87 96.* Open Mon–Fri for lunch and dinner; Sat dinner only. Sleek, beautifully designed restaurant with warm woods, attractive dimmed lighting, and leather chairs. The menu is creative Portuguese.

NEAR LISBON

Cozinha Velha €€€ *Palácio Nacional de Queluz, Largo do Palácio, Queluz. Tel. 21/435 02 32.* Open daily for lunch and dinner. Atmospheric restaurant in former kitchen of the royal palace. Excellent regional cooking.

Colares Velho €€–€€€ *Largo Dr. Carlos França, 1-4, Colares (Sintra). Tel. 21/929 24 06.* Open daily for lunch and dinner. Charming restaurant in small village down the mountain road from Sintra. Imaginative menu with good daily specials. Good value.

ESTREMADURA AND RIBATEJO

Bela Vista €€ *Rua Fonte do Choupo 6, Tomar; Tel. 249/31 28 70.* Closed Mon night, Tues, and all of November. Old house with great views of historic Tomar from across the river. Outdoor terrace in summer. Try the frango à caril (curried chicken).

Calça Perra. €€ *Rua Pedro Dias, 59. Tel. 249/32 16 16.* Closed Wed. Fashionable, friendly 2nd-story restaurant near the synagogue, serving well-prepared fish and meat dishes, including good-value daily lunch specials.

Pousada do Castelo €€€€ *Paço Real, Óbidos. Tel. 262/95 91 05.* Open daily for lunch and dinner. Delightful restaurant within historic Óbidos pousada in medieval castle. Good regional cooking, including specialties like braised kid and asparagus with ham.

Restaurante Tia Alice €€€ Rua do Adro, Fátima. Tel. 249/53 17 37. Closed Sun night and Mon, all of July. Charming, rustic eatery in old house. Açorda (egg and vegetable dish), goat stew, and cod with béchamel sauce are the signature dishes.

THE BEIRAS

Arcadas da Capela. €€€€ *Santa Clara, Coimbra. Tel. 239/80 23 80.* Open daily for dinner. Superb continental restaurant in Quinta das Lágrimas hotel. Great Portuguese specialties like deer steak with port wine sauce, extensive wine list, excellent service.

Adega Paço do Conde. € *Rua Paço do Conde, 10. Coimbra. Tel. 239/256 05.* Open Mon–Sat for lunch and dinner. In the commercial area of old town, an extremely popular bargain restaurant for grilled meats and fish. Simple and always packed. No credit cards.

Portugal

Palace Hotel do Buçaco €€–€€€€ *Buçaco Forest. Tel. 231/93 01 01.* Open daily for lunch and dinner. Elegant restaurant in spectacular setting, amid carved Manueline columns and windows of a legendary royal palace (and today hotel). Prix-fixe menus are good but can't compete with dining room.

O Cortiço $–$$ *Rua Augusto Hilário 47, Viseu; Tel. 232/42 38 53.* Atmospheric traditional restaurant in the historic center, with dining rooms on both sides of the street. Regional cuisine and home cooking, heavy on meat and game. House wine served in wooden jugs.

PORTO AND THE DOURO

D' Tonho €€€ *Cais da Ribeira 13-15, Porto. Tel. 223/200 43 07.* Open daily for lunch and dinner. Beautifully located old townhouse on the riverfront. Specializes in seafood as well as local dishes, but sometimes features regional theme weeks. Chic but relaxed. Good wine list.

Portucale €€€ *Rua da Alegria 598, Porto. Tel. 223/57 07 17.* Open daily for lunch and dinner. Famed restaurant with terrific rooftop views of the city. The menu is a mix of French and Portuguese dishes, including lobster thermidor and Porto-style tripe.

Casa Mariazinha. €€ *Rua 1 de Dezembro, 103 (Matosinhos), Porto. Tel. 229/38 46 15.* Open Tues–Sun for lunch and dinner. Terrific simple neighborhood joint with the freshest grilled fish and shellfish in town, including sand crabs. It's a challenge, though: no sign out front (in blue corner house), no menu, no credit cards—but worth it.

Rabelo (Vintage House) €€€–€€€€ *Lugar da Ponte, 5085 Pinhão. Tel. 254/73 02 30.* Open daily for dinner. Elegant restaurant in beautiful hotel. Dining room has vaulted ceilings and wine-harvest murals. Portuguese specialties like sopa de tomate à Portuguesa (tomato soup with poached egg and bread), grilled fish and meats (veal with port wine and mushrooms), and cheeses accompanied by fine wines. Great library bar to retire to for a glass of port.

MINHO

Bagoeira €–€€ *Avenida Sidónio Pais 57, Barcelos; Tel. 253/81 12 36.* Open daily for lunch and dinner. Popular local restaurant with 19th-century décor, packed on market days. Authentic regional fare such as grilled meats and local sweets, like stuffed oranges.

Restaurante De Bouro €€–€€€ *Rua Santo António das Travessas, 30-32, Braga. Tel. 253/261 609.* Open Mon–Sat for dinner. A small, very impressive and professional restaurant in the historic center, housed in a former convent. Try the daily specials or açorda de camarão (a thick shrimp stew), cod with prawns. Fairly priced, with excellent service and cool, minimalist decor.

Pousada de Nossa Senhora de Oliveira €€–€€€ *Largo da Oliveira, Guimarães; Tel. 253/51 41 57.* Open daily for lunch and dinner. The charming dining room, with wood beams, leather chairs, and exposed stone, of the pousada in central Guimarães. Very good Portuguese and international cuisine. Try the bife especial à pousada (châteaubriand).

Pousada Santa Maria do Bouro €€€ *Amares. Tel. 253/37 19 71.* Open daily for lunch and dinner. Stunning, cavernous dining hall in a former Cistercian Monastery (see page 177). Great bar area with giant fireplace. Local dishes like pork loin stew, codfish with cornbread and cabbage, topped off by a massive dessert buffet of regional sweets.

TRÁS-OS-MONTES

Cozinha do Convento (Forte de São Francisco) €€€ *Chaves. Tel. 276/333 700.* Open daily for lunch and dinner. Elegant restaurant in hotel carved out of a 16th-century convent, overlooking large pool. Focuses on reasonably priced regional mountain cusine. Wines are brought up from the extensive cellar in the old cistern. Also a separate, atmospheric tavern for informal meals.

Solar do Bragança. €€ *Praça da Sé, 34, Bragança. Tel. 273/32 38 75.* Open daily for lunch and dinner. Excellent restaurant occupying three rooms of an old noble house on the main square. Elegant but laid-back, with rustic furnishings, chandeliers, and fresh flowers. Several exotic meats, game, and an excellent-value five-course "menu turístico." Highly recommended.

ALENTEJO

São Rosas €€–€€€ *Largo D. Dinis, 11. Estremoz; Tel. 268/33 33 45.* Open daily for lunch and dinner. An elegant but understated restaurant next to the castle pousada with beamed ceilings and earthy furnishings. Local dishes include grilled scabbard fish and roast pork loin with applesauce. Good-value "tourist menu" at both lunch and dinner.

Cozinha de Santo Humberto €€ *Rua da Moeda 39, Évora; Tel. 266/70 42 51.* Open Fri–Wed for lunch and dinner; closed all of November. On a small street off Praça Giraldo, a highly recommended restaurant in an ancient cellar loaded with antiques. Serves classic dishes of the Alentejo and is strong on game dishes, such as wild boar and partridge.

Pousada dos Lóios €€€–€€€€ *Largo Conde de Vila Flor, Évora; Tel. 266/70 40 51.* Open daily for lunch and dinner. Beautiful dining room in the cloister of an old monastery, now a sought-after pousada (see page 178). Serves a varied selection of regional Alentejano cuisine, such as codfish with coriander, fish soup with mint, and other unique Portuguese dishes.

O Ermita €€€€ *Aldeia da Serra, Redondo. Tel. 266/98 91 60.* Open daily for lunch and dinner. In an isolated 12th-century convent (Hotel Convento de São Paulo), an exquisite restaurant with vaulted ceilings, 18th-century frescoes, and beautiful azulejos. Many Portuguese drive out for a special occasion. Alentejo specialties.

THE ALGARVE

Grand Café €€–€€€ *Rua Senhora da Graça, 2, Lagos; Tel. 282/702 622.* Open daily for lunch and dinner. Most inventive restaurant in town, with eclectic menu, daily specials, outdoor terrace, and funky interior with a cool bar open late.

Restaurante Casa Amélia €–€€ *Cais da Lota, Loja 3, Portimão. Tel. 914/706 865.* Open Tues–Sun for lunch and dinner. One of the informal restaurants lining the quayside in Portimão. Specializing in grilled sardines and other grilled seafood. No credit cards.

Restaurante Atlántida €€–€€€ *Praia de Tres Irmãos; Tel. 282/459 647.* Open daily for lunch and dinner. Terrific fish shack right on the beach, below the Carlton Alvor hotel. Fresh fish direct from the boats. Romantic deck.

Restaurante do Hotel Villa Joya €€€€ *in Hotel Villa Joya, Praia de Galé; Tel. 289/591 795.* Open daily for dinner; closed in November and January. Refined and elegant hotel restaurant preparing eclectic international dishes. Reservations for non-guests essential.

Casa Velha €€€€ Quinta do Lago (Almancil); Tel. 289/394 983. Open Mon–Sat for dinner. Chic restaurant in a renovated 19th-century farmhouse; about as elegant as dining in the Algarve gets. French menu and excellent wine cellar.

Quatro Águas €€€ *Rua Domingos Guieiro 19 (Tavira). Tel. 289/827 145.* Open daily for lunch and dinner; closed Mon. during winter. Handsome 18th-century building on the harbor. Traditional Portuguese dining, with an emphasis on seafood dishes like arroz de marisco (seafood rice) and octopus stew.

INDEX